FORTRESS • 75

THE FORTS OF NEW FRANCE

in Northeast America 1600–1763

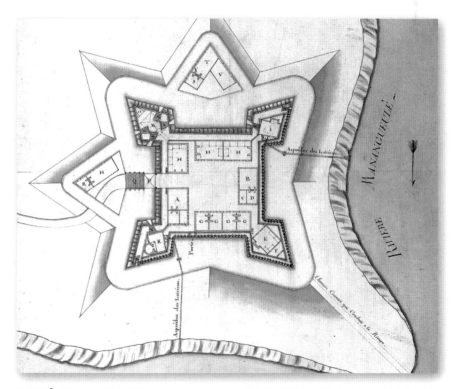

RENÉ CHARTRAND

ILLUSTRATED BY BRIAN DELF

Series editors Marcus Cowper and Nikolai Bogdanovic

First published in Great Britain in 2008 by Osprey Publishing,
Midland House, West Way, Botley, Oxford OX2 0PH, UK
443 Park Avenue South, New York, NY 10016, USA
Email: info@ospreypublishing.com

A CIP catalog record for this book is available from the British Library.

ISBN-13 978 1 84603 255 4

Editorial by Ilios Publishing, Oxford, UK (www.iliospublishing.com)
Page layout by Ken Vail Graphic Design, Cambridge, UK (kvgd.com)
Cartography: Map Studio, Romsey, UK
Typeset in Sabon and Myriad Pro
Index by Alison Worthington
Originated by PPS Grasmere Ltd, Leeds, UK
Printed and bound in China through Bookbuilders

08 09 10 11 12   10 9 8 7 6 5 4 3 2 1

FOR A CATALOG OF ALL BOOKS PUBLISHED BY OSPREY MILITARY
AND AVIATION PLEASE CONTACT:

NORTH AMERICA
Osprey Direct, c/o Random House Distribution Center, 400 Hahn Road,
Westminster, MD 21157
Email: info@ospreydirect.com

ALL OTHER REGIONS
Osprey Direct UK, PO Box 140, Wellingborough,
Northants, NN8 2FA, UK
Email: info@ospreydirect.co.uk

www.ospreypublishing.com

AUTHOR'S NOTE

This work, the first of a two-part series, is the companion of *French
Fortresses in North America 1535–1763* (Fortress 27) that dealt with the
fortified cities of Québec, Montréal, Louisbourg, and New Orleans. We
continue our studies by presenting the numerous military forts that the
French built in North America. As will be seen, individual forts spread across
the continent rarely existed by themselves but instead formed part of a
defense scheme in which trade and colonization were determining factors.
Therefore, except for 16th-century structures, we present the forts by area.
This first part will concentrate on forts on the Atlantic Coast and on the St
Lawrence, Richelieu, Ohio, and Ottawa river valleys. The second part will
deal with forts of the Great Lakes, the Mississippi Valley, and the Gulf of
Mexico. Thus, it is hoped that, when completed, these three Osprey Fortress
books will form the most important illustrated account yet published of
New France's truly extraordinary fortifications.

The author wishes to acknowledge the very kind assistance of Christopher
D. Fox of Fort Ticonderoga, the staff (amongst whom are many former
colleagues) at forts administered by the National Historic Sites of Parks
Canada, the staff at the Library and Archives Canada in Ottawa, Crown
Point State Historic Site, and at the Fort Pitt Museum in Pittsburgh.

Unless accompanied by a negative number or otherwise indicated, all
photos are by the author.

MEASUREMENTS

Unless otherwise indicated, we have given French feet and inches as they
appeared in the 17th- and 18th-century documentation. It is most
important to note that the French foot, used in New France, was not the
same as the English foot (still officially used in the United States). The
French 12 inches is longer and comes to 12.789 inches, English measure.

The official French measures from 1668–1840 were:

2 miles for 1 Lieue = 3.898 km
1000 Toises for 1 mile = 1.949 km (English mile = 1.61 km)
6 feet for 1 Toise = 1.949 m (English Fathom = 1.83 m)
12 inches for 1 foot = 32.484 cm (English foot = 30.48 cm)
12 lines for 1 inch = 2.707 cm (English inch = 2.54 cm)

ARTIST'S NOTE

Readers may care to note that the original paintings from which the
color plates in this book were prepared are available for private sale.
All reproduction copyright whatsoever is retained by the Publishers.
All enquiries should be addressed to:

Brian Delf, 7 Burcot Park, Burcot, Abingdon OX14 3DH, UK

The Publishers regret that they can enter into no correspondence upon
this matter.

THE FORTRESS STUDY GROUP (FSG)

The object of the FSG is to advance the education of the public in the study
of all aspects of fortifications and their armaments, especially works
constructed to mount or resist artillery. The FSG holds an annual
conference in September over a long weekend with visits and evening
lectures, an annual tour abroad lasting about eight days, and an annual
Members' Day.

The FSG journal, *FORT*, is published annually, and its newsletter, *Casemate*,
is published three times a year. Membership is international. For further
details, please contact:

The Secretary, c/o 6 Lanark Place, London W9 1BS, UK

Web site: www.fsgfort.com

THE WOODLAND TRUST

Osprey Publishing are supporting the Woodland Trust, the UK's leading
woodland conservation charity, by funding the dedication of trees.

CONTENTS

THE FORTS OF NEW FRANCE IN NORTHEAST AMERICA 1600–1763

INTRODUCTION

During the 16th century, the various French attempts to establish settlements in North and South America all failed. It was during the 17th century that France at last managed to establish a domain in what is now eastern Canada. The first half of the 17th century saw a number of relatively small forts, or fortified settlements, established on the Atlantic Coast and on the shores of the St Lawrence River. This was a period of extraordinary explorations that saw adventurous men such as Samuel de Champlain or Etienne Brûlé reveal the existence of the Great Lakes and of great rivers in the interior of the North American continent. The rivers would prove to be the key to the ever-expanding domain claimed by France. During the second half of the 17th century, French explorers reached the edge of the western prairies, Hudson's Bay, and in 1682, Robert Cavalier de La Salle reached the Gulf of Mexico by going down the Mississippi River. Explorations farther west by Pierre Gaulthier de La Vérendrye and his sons continued during the 1730s, revealing an enormous domain whose limit was finally reached in January 1743 when, in the present-day US state of Wyoming, the mighty Rocky Mountains stopped further westward advances. The essential geographical boundaries of New France in North America were thus reached.

To secure all these areas, the French built a large number of forts along the shores of the lakes and waterways of their trade network routes. The forts were basically laid out in a square plan with bastions of various sizes. However, the similarities with small forts in Europe were likely to end there.

Detail of a map of New France showing French troops bearing pikes and a unit color (left) with the Seigneur de Roberval in armor during his 1542–1543 expedition. To the left of Roberval is a small rendering of the fort of France-Roy, symbolically shown as a stone castle having two turrets with a wall and a gate. The natives are also generically shown naked with furs. It must be stressed that illustrations of the 16th and part of the 17th centuries were meant to be an evocation rather than a precise rendering of persons and places. This 1546 map by Pierre Decellier has north at the bottom and south at the top. Library and Archives Canada, NMC 40461.

The type of fort put up in New France could have substantial variations depending on its purpose. Coastal forts such as those at Port Royal or Placentia were mostly concerned with attacks from ships and would have cannon batteries and earthen works. As one moved into the continent's interior, the forts would be made of timber planted in the ground to make palisades; this was because it was taken for granted that moving a heavy artillery train in the wilderness was next to impossible and that Indian enemies did not use ordnance. However, as time passed, the need to have substantial and impressive-looking stone fortifications along the most likely interior invasion route into Canada, the Lake Champlain and the Richelieu River corridor, became increasingly important. Thus, when Fort Chambly was rebuilt in the early 18th century, it assumed the appearance of a somewhat medieval stone fort with high walls and massive corner turrets. This followed a recommendation by Marshal Vauban himself, and a similarly imposing type of stone fort was repeated when Fort Saint-Frédéric (Crown Point, NY) was built with its large tower.

Captain Jacques Cartier taking possession of Canada for France by erecting a cross bearing a shield with the royal arms at Gaspé in 1534. He named the area New France. This type of ceremony was repeated in various places in the following years and decades. Plate after René Bombled. Private collection.

This style rapidly evolved into the more standard design of fort built on a square plan with sizable bastions mounted with ordnance at each corner by the middle of the 18th century. This was the type of fort built by the French as they advanced into the Ohio Valley and toward Lake Champlain. Its most "finished" example was Fort Carillon (Ticonderoga, NY) built below Lake Champlain from 1755, which was to be reveted with stone. During the 1750s, several fort designs were tried out. The "star" design was used when Fort Beauséjour was built. Later, as invading Anglo-American armies in overwhelming numbers were closing in, structures that were designed primarily to be powerful batteries, such as forts Isle-aux-Noix, Lévis, or Jacques-Cartier, were built. Thus, it can be seen that engineers serving in New France tried nearly all types of fortifications in the northeastern part of North America.

CHRONOLOGY

1534	Explorer Jacques Cartier takes possession of Canada for France at Gaspé. The area is named New France.
1535	Cartier and his men build a small fort in the area of Québec.
1541–1543	Cartier and the Seigneur de Roberval build forts at Cap-Rouge near Québec, but the colony is abandoned in 1543.
1555–1560	French settlement in Brazil; destroyed by Portuguese.
1562–1565	French settlements in Florida; destroyed by Spanish.
1598–1603	Sable Island (Nova Scotia) settlement fails.
1600–1601	Fortified post at Tadoussac.
1604–1605	Fortified post at Isle Sainte-Croix, Acadia.
1605	Port Royal, Acadia, habitation built, destroyed in 1613.
1608	Samuel de Champlain, explorer and first governor of New France, founds Québec.

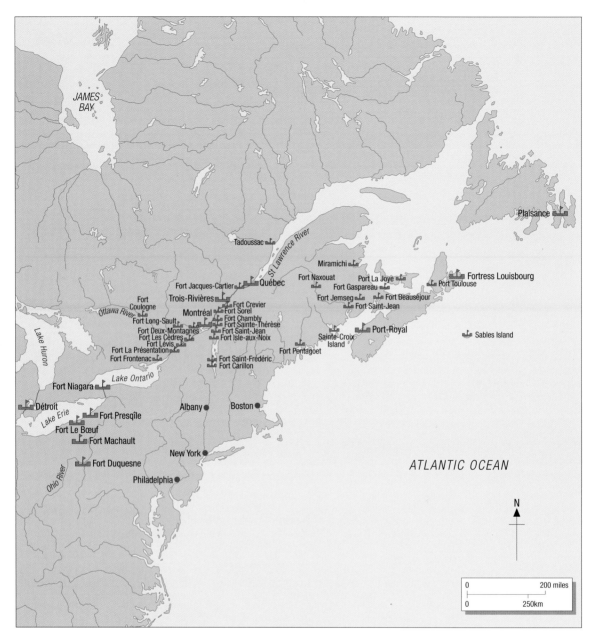

A map of the French forts and settlements in northeastern America that had military garrisons. Some forts had several names, and were reconstructed over the years.

1630s	Permanent settlements in Acadia; several forts built.
1632	Trois-Rivières founded.
1642	Fort Richelieu built at mouth of Richelieu River; Montréal, originally named Ville-Marie, is founded.
1662	Placentia, Newfoundland, settled permanently by the French.
1665–1666	Forts Sorel, Chambly, Saint-Jean, Sainte-Thérèse built on Richelieu River.
1670s–1690s	Many seigneurial forts built, especially east of Montréal.
1686	First of many successful Canadian and French expeditions to capture and hold British forts in Hudson's Bay. Forts built on the Ottawa River.

1699	First permanent French settlements in Louisiana.
1701	Great Peace of Montréal between French and Indians.
1710	Port Royal, Acadia, falls to Anglo-Americans.
1713	Treaty of Utrecht cedes Acadia (Nova Scotia), Placentia, and Hudson's Bay forts to Great Britain.
1720	Foundation stone is laid at Louisbourg, and extensive fortifications are built there. French settle Ile-Saint-Jean (now Prince Edward Island).
1731	Fort at Pointe à la Chevelure (Crown Point, NY) built, renamed Saint-Frédéric in 1738.
1745	Louisbourg falls to a New England army.
1748	Fort Saint-Jean and Fort La Présentation built.
1749	Louisbourg returned to the French.
1751	Forts Beauséjour and Gaspareau built.
1753	Forts Presqu'île, Le Boeuf, and Machault built.
1754	Fort Duquesne built.
1755	Fort Beauséjour and Gaspareau taken by Anglo-Americans.
	July: General Braddock defeated at Monongahela near Fort Duquesne.
	September: Fort Carillon built at Ticonderoga.
1756	Montcalm takes Oswego.
1757	Montcalm takes Fort William-Henry.
1758	**July 8:** British defeated at Ticonderoga by Montcalm.
	July: Louisbourg falls to British Army and fleet.
	November: Fort Duquesne evacuated and blown up by French.
1759	Forts Carillon and Saint-Frédéric evacuated and blown up by French.
	September 13: French Army defeated on the Plains of Abraham, Montcalm and Wolfe killed; Québec City surrenders September 18.
	Forts Isle-aux-Noix, Lévis, and Jacques-Cartier built.
1760	**April–May:** French siege to retake Québec fails.
	August: Isle-aux-Noix and Fort Lévis fall to British.
	Last French army in Canada surrenders at Montréal on September 8.
	Fort Jacques-Cartier surrenders on September 10.
1763	Treaty of Paris: France cedes Canada, Isle Royale, and Louisiana on east side of Mississippi River to Britain, rest of Louisiana to Spain.

The French naval ensign used until 1661

This flag consisted of a white cross on a blue background, although in the 16th century, this flag had some variations such as blue and red quarters. It could also be hoisted on coastal forts such as the early settlements built by the French in the early 17th century. It was gradually replaced by the white ensign used on French warships. In 1661, King Louis XIV officially replaced it with the white ensign for ships of war, keeping this blue ensign as the merchant marine flag with the addition of the royal coat of arms at its center. Private collection.

A TOUR OF THE FORTS

16th-century forts

The earliest French forts in America were built in 1535 at the foot of Cape Diamond and in 1541 at Cap-Rouge, about 14 km (8.7 mi) west of the present city of Québec. That year, a major expedition to Canada was being prepared in France. Following the explorations by Jacques Cartier in 1534 and 1535, King François I appointed one of his courtiers, Jean-François de La Roque, Seigneur de Roberval, as governor and lieutenant general of a colony to be established on the shores of the St Lawrence River. Jacques Cartier was captain general and master pilot of the fleet with authority to command in the absence of Roberval. There were various delays, so that in May 1541, Cartier left Saint-Malo for Canada with a fleet of five ships carrying gentlemen, settlers, soldiers, convicts, and supplies for two years. After a stormy crossing, they reached the area of present-day Québec City in late August. Cartier felt that the best spot for the settlement was at the foot of the Cap-Rouge River. He landed his artillery from three of his ships (the place was named Charlebourg-Royal after the king's third son), and two forts were built, one at the foot of the cliff and one on top of it. The settlement failed owing to the hostility of the Indians, and the settlement was abandoned, with Cartier and the settlers going back to France in late spring 1542. Meanwhile, Roberval had sailed from France with 200 men and arrived at Cap-Rouge at the end of July. The two destroyed forts were rebuilt and the place renamed France-Roy. These settlers had no better luck with the natives, and scurvy decimated the French during the winter. In spring 1543, Roberval and the survivors abandoned the place and went back to France. As noted in *French Fortresses in North America 1535–1763* (Osprey Fortress 27), the descriptions of these forts were very vague. Only Roberval's forts are recorded. The smaller one on the cliff, with a large tower and a main building, was said to be very strong. The one at the foot of the cliff had a tower two stories high and two main buildings. In about 1860, some foundations were found at Cap-Rouge that might have belonged to the long-vanished lower fort, but nothing could confirm this theory.

Then, on August 19, 2006, the prime minister of Québec announced a stunning discovery: the remains of this 16th-century settlement had been found at Cap-Rouge. During a routine archeological survey undertaken before construction began, archeologist Yves Chrétien came upon some very unusual objects including fragments of very early Italian and Indian pottery.

Construction of Fort Caroline, Florida, during 1564, on the banks of the present St John's River, near Jacksonville. Work started on June 30. "Having measured a triangular space" some settlers cut wood for fascines while others moved the sandy soil "to give a shape to the rampart" that was 9 ft high, wrote Commandant René de Laudonnière. This print, after Jacques Le Moyne, is one of very few that shows the construction of a fort. Private collection.

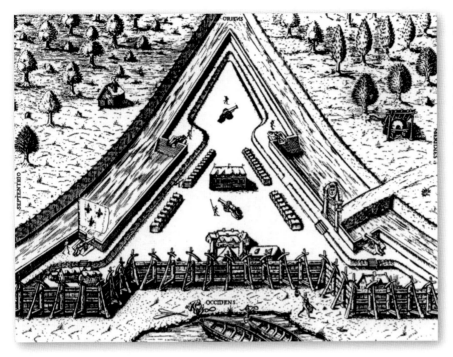

Fort Caroline, Florida, as completed in 1564. Each end of its triangular plan had a bastion mounted with artillery, the westward sides facing the mainland having a moat outside, and the east side facing the river having a palisade "in the manner that gabions are made." The fortification "was made of fascines and sand except up to two or three feet at top of grass [sods], of which the parapets were made." The ammunition magazine was in the south bastion (lower left) with the French flag. The house at the center was the commandant's. The fort was taken by the Spanish on September 20, 1565, and its "French Lutheran" garrison put to the sword. Print after Jacques Le Moyne, a colonist who escaped the massacre. Private collection.

After careful analysis of the objects including extensive carbon 14 tests, the only conclusion possible was that it was the site of the 1541–1543 forts. This was a very important discovery indeed as it is the second-oldest European site, after the Viking site of L'Anse aux Meadows (c. AD 1000) in Newfoundland, to be discovered in North America. Millions of dollars are being invested in further archeological work at the site so that, in several years, we may have a better idea of what these forts were like.

France's next endeavors in America came from its numerous Protestant communities. Admiral Gaspard de Coligny, the leader of the Protestants as well as one of the most powerful people in the realm, had visions of an overseas France, and in 1555, mooted the settlement of a Protestant colony in Brazil, a country that belonged to Portugal. A fleet sailed in July under the command of the vice admiral of Brittany, Nicolas Druand de Villegagnon, and landed at what is now Rio de Janeiro, in November. The French Protestants settled on an island in the bay and there built Fort Coligny as well as a battery on a smaller island. The Portuguese were none too pleased at these new settlers, and on March 15, 1560, took the place and razed the fort after a three-week siege.

But the Protestants did not give up on the idea of settlement. In May 1562, a group under Jean Ribault composed of about 150 gentlemen and "old soldiers" arrived at the present Port Royal Sound, South Carolina, and built Charlesfort in the area of Parris Island or Beaufort Island. It was built on a

Champlain's Explorations

The French expansion from the small 1608 post at Québec to an empire that spanned North America's interior from the Gulf of St Lawrence to the Gulf of Mexico was due to the initial explorations of Samuel de Champlain, first governor of New France. Champlain first went south beyond Lake Champlain in 1609, then, in 1613, found the way to Lake Huron by the Ottawa River that would open up the main fur trade route; two years later, he ventured south of Lake Ontario. On two occasions he fought the Iroquois, who would become New France's enemies in the 17th century. These and later explorations resulted in many French forts being erected in North America's hinterland. Map after C. W. Jefferys.

The 11 survivors of the 1598 settlement on Sable Island rescued by Captain Chefdhostel in 1603. Following an earlier mutiny in which Commandant Querbonyer and several other men were killed, the survivors were reduced to utmost misery. When found, they were haggard, had long hair and beards, and wore animal hides as shown in the plate after René Bombled. Intrigued by this event, King Henri IV asked to see these former convicts (and possibly soldiers). Judging that fate had punished them amply, they were sent home with part of the profit from the pelts and whale oil found on the island. Private collection.

slightly rectangular plan, its dimensions being 16 by 13 phantoms (96 × 78 ft; 29.2 × 23.7 m). It was described as "a blockhouse of log and clay, thatched with straw, with a ditch around it, with four bastions, and two bronze falconets and six iron culverins therein." Ribault went back to France, leaving 30 men there who were all but abandoned because of the misfortunes besetting Ribault. The Spanish realized they were there, and on June 12, 1564, attacked and razed Charlesfort. Meanwhile, a fleet of three ships under René Goulaine de Laudonnière was sent out by Admiral Coligny in 1564, and in July, built Fort Caroline, named in honor of King Charles IX, at the mouth of the St John's River in northern Florida. It was an earth and log fort built on a triangular plan with small bastions at each corner.

Initial good relations with the Indians turned sour, and by 1565, the French were at war with the indigenous groups in the area. The Spanish had also learned of the new French Protestant fort and were determined to wipe it out. One of their best fleet commanders, Pedro Menendez de Aviles, was sent from Spain with ten ships bearing 820 soldiers for the task. After a stop farther south, where he founded St Augustine, he marched to Fort Caroline and took it by storm on September 20, killing all the "French Lutheran" men. The fort itself was renamed San Mateo and was occupied by the Spanish. The French vowed revenge for the massacres, and on April 26, 1568, Dominique de Gourgues and a strong body of French Protestant corsairs took Fort San Mateo, razed the place, and hung all the Spanish male prisoners. Thus ended the tragic episode of French colonization in Florida.

For the next few decades, French traders, corsairs, and fishermen often cruised off the North American coast, but no further attempts at settlement were made until 1598. That year, the Marquis de La Roche landed about 40 colonists, recruited in French prisons and escorted by about ten soldiers, on Sable Island, off the coast of the present Canadian province of Nova Scotia. Lodgings and a storehouse were built, and there were some probably some defensive structures, most likely moats and earthen works, as Sable Island was (and remains) sandy and devoid of trees. By 1603, only 11 survivors remained to be rescued, the rest having perished in a mutiny that probably occurred the previous year.

Meanwhile, as French merchant ships often went up the St Lawrence River to trade with the Indians, Pierre Chauvin de Tonnetuit landed men and supplies at Tadoussac in 1600 and proceeded to build a "habitation" (a strongly built house) there, which had some defensive features. The 16 men left there spent a disastrous winter beset by sickness and starvation. Some died, and the rest went back to France in spring 1601, abandoning the habitation. Thus, all the French settlement attempts during the 16th century had ended in failure.

Early Construction Techniques

The earliest palisades for defense and their auxiliary buildings were constructed by the *en pile* method of setting logs into the ground. More substantial buildings were made with logs laid horizontally and notched at the corners. The earliest type of semi-permanent lodging consisted of a frame built of long, squared timbers with walls made of shorter logs that might be covered by planks. Print after C. W. Jefferys. Private collection.

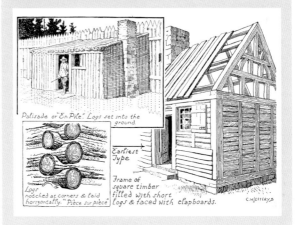

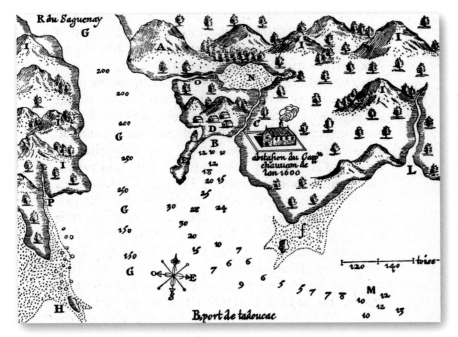

The bay of Tadoussac with the habitation built by Pierre Chauvin de Tonnetuit in 1600. At left, the Saguenay River flows south into the St Lawrence. According to Champlain, the habitation at Tadoussac was small, measuring 7.8 x 5.8 m (8.5x6.3 yd) and 2.6 m (2.8 yd) high. Its defensive features seem to have been minimal as it was surrounded only by a picket fence and a "small [or shallow] ditch dug in the sand." The little houses marked "D" were the Indians' huts. Map from *Champlain's Voyages*.

The 1604 settlement on Sainte-Croix Island. It was built on an island in the middle of the Sainte-Croix River, which is now the border between the US state of Maine and the Canadian province of New Brunswick. The house at top left (D) was the "lodging of the Swiss", soldier-artisans that were part of the expedition. The storehouse (C) was surrounded by a palisade. Champlain mentioned that the first structure put up on the island was a "barricade" that "served as a platform to place our cannon," which is not shown as it was to the south (bottom) of the settlement. The squared timber buildings on Sainte-Croix Island were dismantled in 1605 and transported to Port Royal to build the habitation there. Plate from *Champlain's Voyages*.

Forts on the Atlantic

At the beginning of the 17th century, French merchants were confident that a lucrative trade could be entered into with the native inhabitants of the northeastern part of America. Since Jacques Cartier's explorations in the 1530s, France had a solid claim to this part of America, and it was felt in the court of King Henri IV that some establishments would soon have to be made before competing nations set up their own colonies in that part of the continent. Royal charters were thus granted to groups of merchants willing to risk capital in such ventures. In the case of Nova Scotia/Acadia, both the kings of France and England granted charters.

The Port Royal habitation built in 1605. It had a rectangular plan, its timber buildings acting as defensive walls, and it also featured a platform "with four guns" according to Champlain, although he shows only three (B), a palisade redoubt (F), and a ditch (M). The artisans were lodged on the left side (A), and the storehouse was on the right side (C). The rest of the quarters were for the officers (O, N, and D), and also shown are a forge (E), an oven, and a kitchen (G and H). It also had "a very good basement 4–5 ft high." This habitation was destroyed by English corsairs from Virginia in November 1613. Plate from *Champlain's Voyages*.

Acadia in 1609 as depicted by Marc Lescarbot, a member of the Port Royal colony. This detail from his map shows what is now the present US state of Maine (on the left). Near the center is Sainte-Croix Island, site of the first settlement in 1604, and now the border between Maine and the Canadian province of New Brunswick. The 1605 Port Royal settlement is at the center on the "Souriquois" peninsula, now mainland Nova Scotia, and "Bacaillos" is Cape Breton Island. Just below is "I de sable" – the site of the doomed Sable Island colony in 1598.

In 1603, Pierre Dugua de Mons received from King Henri IV of France a fur trade monopoly for a large area in northeastern North America. His expedition arrived in 1604 and selected Sainte-Croix Island for settlement. That winter, many colonists perished from scurvy, and the following summer, Samuel de Champlain, the expedition's explorer and mapmaker, selected a new site. The colony moved to Port-Royal (Annapolis Royal, Nova Scotia), across the Bay of Fundy, and built a habitation there. In November 1613, the place was attacked and destroyed by an English expedition from Virginia led by Samuel Argall, who had been commissioned to expel all Frenchmen from territory claimed by King James I of England.

In reality, the area remained devoid of European trade posts or settlements until Charles Saint-Etienne de la Tour built Fort Saint-Louis (Port La Tour, Nova Scotia), also known as Fort Lomeron, in 1623. The fort was attacked by the British in 1629 and 1630, and it was abandoned in 1635. Nicolas Denys built the trade fort Sainte-Anne (Englishtown, Nova Scotia) that operated from 1629 to 1641. In 1632, Fort Ste Marie de Grace (La Havre, Nova Scotia) was built by Isaac de Razilly, who was appointed "governor of New France" by King Louis XIII; it served as the first capital of New France until abandoned in 1636.

Meanwhile, Scottish settlers arrived in 1629 on the abandoned site of Port Royal and built "Charles Fort" there, but it was attacked and taken by the French in 1632. The Treaty of Aix-la-Chapelle granted Canada and Acadia to France, and French colonists replaced the Scots at Port Royal, which became the capital from 1636. The first French fort at Port Royal was built

The Port Royal area. The first habitation (1605–1613) was built on the shore of what is now known as the Annapolis Basin facing Goat Island (top). The short-lived Scottish settlement's fort (1630) was put up near the same site. The second Port Royal was built farther in the basin on the opposite shore (right). It was renamed Annapolis Royal by the British in 1710. The access to the sea is through the Digby Gut (upper left). Detail from map by C. W. Jefferys.

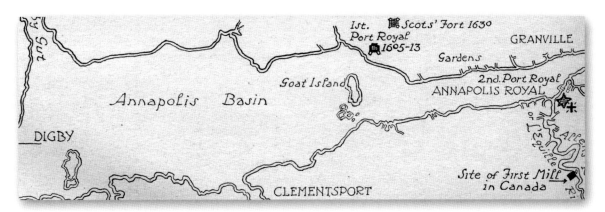

The fort at Port Royal, Acadia, c. 1706–1710

The 1702–1703 plan to build a substantial fort at Port Royal featured a large semicircular battery near the water. This feature was not approved by Seigneur de Subercase, commanding officer at Port Royal, who had a large triangular ravelin built instead, with guns installed to face the water. The fort was built on a slight height at Port Royal's entrance on a square plan with four bastions. It had a residence for the governor of Acadia as well as quarters for the officers and men of the garrison. This fort was sufficiently strong to repulse Anglo-American attacks in 1704 and 1707, but it finally surrendered in October 1710 to overwhelming British and colonial American forces.

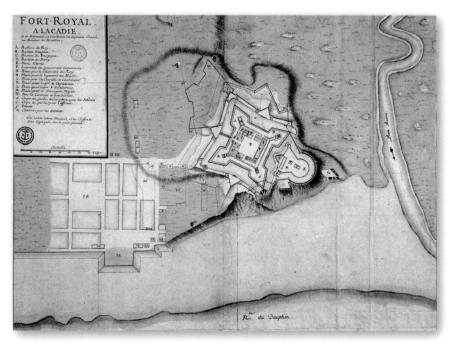

FORT·ROYAL. A·LACADIE

R.^u du Dauphin.

Plan of the fort at Port Royal in 1703. This plan showed what had been built since 1702 or was being constructed and made proposals for other structures as shown in various outlines. The most important proposal was an outside circular battery on the left of the fort facing the shore. An outside battery was indeed built but it did not have this shape. The main parts of the fort were: A: du Roy bastion; B: Dauphin bastion; C: Bourgogne bastion; D: Berry bastion; E: parade; F: governor's residence; G: king's lieutenant's quarters; H: major's quarters; I: chapel and chaplain's quarters; K and L: officers' quarters; M: surgeon's quarters; N: gunners' quarters. The town and its docks are shown at bottom left. Archives Nationales, Dépôt des Fortifications des Colonies.

at that time and probably incorporated part of the previous Scottish fort. Over the years, two other rather makeshift forts were constructed on the site, but they gradually fell into disrepair. De Meule's plan of Port Royal shows that by 1686 there was no fort to defend the place, and it was easily captured and occupied briefly by Sir William Phips in early 1690.

In 1702, construction started on a substantial Vauban-style earthwork fort built on a square plan with bastions, ditches, and glacis with a large ravelin to cover the gate. It repulsed Anglo-American attacks in 1704 and 1707, but it finally surrendered in October 1710 to overwhelming British and colonial American forces. The British occupied the fort and town, which they renamed Fort Anne and Annapolis Royal respectively, in honor of Queen Anne of Great Britain. Acadia was ceded to Britain in 1713 and became Nova Scotia.

Not all of Acadia/Nova Scotia went to Britain. France kept Cape Breton Island, renamed Isle Royale, Isle Saint-Jean (now the Canadian province of Prince Edward Island), and what is now eastern New Brunswick. Fortress Louisbourg on Cape Breton Island was built and quickly became one of the most important harbors on the eastern seaboard. However, it

The fort's powder magazine built from 1702 at Port Royal, Acadia. Print after C. W. Jefferys.

was taken in 1745 and again in 1758 and later razed. Elsewhere on Cape Breton Island, a settlement was made from 1713 at Port Toulouse (now St Peters, 120 km [74.6 mi] from Louisbourg) where there had been the small fortified fur post named Saint-Pierre between the 1630s and 1669. To protect the new settlement and transportation across the isthmus, the French built a small fort there armed with six 6-pdrs in 1715–1716. A small garrison was maintained. A larger earthwork fort surrounded by a ditch was built between 1734 and 1738 near the shore. It had two bastions facing land with a curved barbette battery facing the harbor. Both the fort and the settlement were destroyed by Anglo-American troops in 1745 after the surrender of Louisbourg. It was reoccupied between 1749 and 1758, but no substantial fortifications were rebuilt there. Another settlement with a small detachment of troops was at Port Dauphin on the north end of the island, which was briefly the capital of Isle Royale from 1713 to 1719 when officials moved to Louisbourg. There were plans to build a fort there, as shown on Bellin's 1744 map, but nothing important was actually built.

Acadian Borderlands

Acadia extended beyond present-day Nova Scotia. From the second quarter of the 17th century, settlements, missions, and outposts were made in the present-day US state of Maine and the Canadian provinces of New Brunswick and Prince Edward Island.

The earliest post was Fort Pentagoet (Castine, Maine) also known as Fort Penobscot, which was first established as a Dutch trading station in 1613 and later abandoned. Champlain had explored the Penobscot Bay area earlier, but in 1614, Captain John Smith charted it for England. It thus became, like much of Acadia, an area of conflicting territorial claims. In 1629, Pilgrim colonists from Massachusetts established a fortified trading post there flying the flag of England. The French felt usurped, and in 1634 they seized the place. Their early fort was more of a trading post than with a number of Indian settlements nearby than a military installation. In 1654, it was captured by Anglo-Americans from Massachusetts who occupied it until 1670 when the place was returned to France following the Treaty of Breda. A stronger-bastioned fort was built by Jean Vincent d'Abbadie, Baron de Saint-Castin, who was granted the land in the

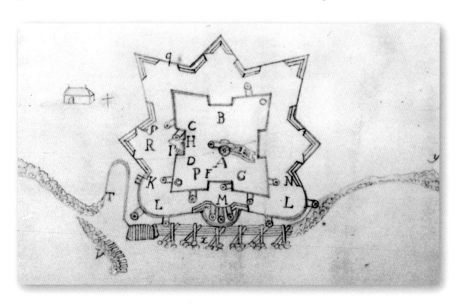

C.W. JEFFERYS

vicinity of Pentagoet by the King of France, hence the later name of Castine. The fort was taken and sacked by Dutch corsairs in 1674. Two years later, they Dutch were back and bombarded the fort until it was destroyed. Saint-Castin and his son had forged strong alliances with the Micmac Indians, living among them as chiefs, and thereafter occasionally used some of the abandoned structures as a supply base for raiding parties on northern New England. In 1688, Anglo-Americans razed what remained and permanently occupied the area.

Fort La Tour (St John, New Brunswick) was built as a fortified trading post during 1635. It likely was reinforced in the years to come as the Seigneur de La Tour and the Seigneur de Charnisay became embroiled in a violent dispute over conflicting territorial claims, each claiming to be the ruler of the area. In 1645, De Charnisay and a superior force attacked Fort La Tour. La Tour was absent, but his wife led a vigorous defense, although eventually she had to

PLAN ET VEUE DU FORT
Sᵗ IOSEPH
fur la Riviere Sᵗ Iean
A L'ACADIE :

17

Fort Beauséjour, 1751–1755

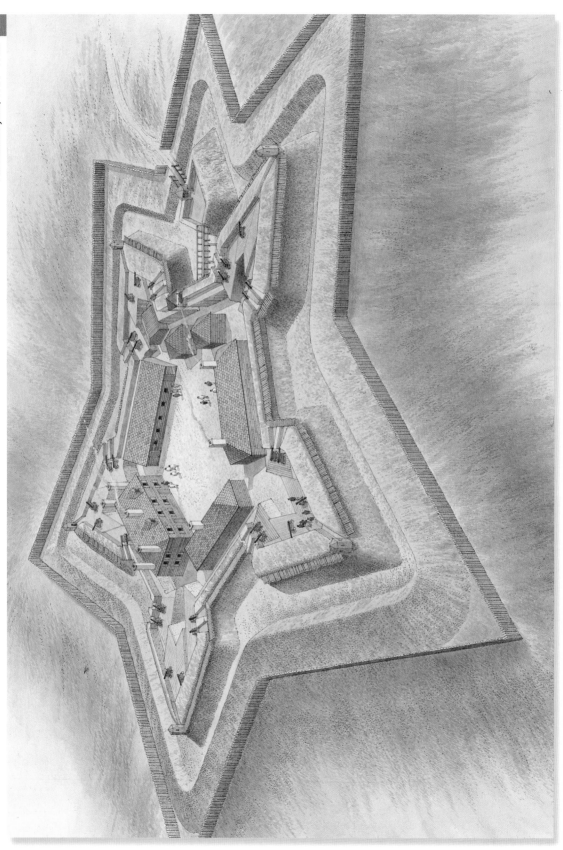

B FORT BEAUSÉJOUR, 1751–1755

Built of earth and wood, this fort was laid out on a pentagonal "star" plan with five bastions rather than the usual square with four bastions to take maximum advantage of the height on which it was built. The pentagon's ramparts were about 3 m (9.8 English feet) high. The face of the bastions was 17.5 m (57.4 English feet), the flanks 5.8 m (19 English feet), and the connecting curtain wall 21.2 m (69.5 English feet),

although these measurements were not absolute and could vary. The ditch was 5.5 m (18 English feet) wide × 2 m (6.6 English feet) deep and had a glacis farther out. The well, powder magazine, and all the planned buildings except the barracks were built by the end of 1751, with the barracks being finished the following year. It was taken by an Anglo-American force in June 1755.

surrender. She was then forced to watch the execution of part of her garrison; she died a few weeks later. Fort Charnisay was built in the late 1640s. The Anglo-Americans occupied the area in 1654. Following the cession of these territories to France by treaty, the fort, which had been allowed to fall into disrepair, was rebuilt and renamed Fort Martignon in 1672. Over the years, this fort also fell into neglect.

Fort Jemseg (or Jemseck) was built by the Anglo-Americans in 1659 at the confluence of the St John and Jemseg rivers. It was ceded to France, and a small garrison was sent there in 1670, but it was taken by the Dutch in 1674 and abandoned. In 1690, Governor de Villebon had it repaired but found it unsuitable and moved farther north two years later.

In 1692, De Villebon had a fort built at the meeting of the St John and Nashwaak rivers (now Fredericton, New Brunswick). Work started on March 8, St Joseph's Day, so it was christened Fort Saint-Joseph, but it was also known as Fort Nashwaak or Fort Naxouat. This fort was occupied until 1698 when De Villebon left it to build another fort at the mouth of the St John River.

Fort Saint-Jean, also known as Fort Villebon and Fort Menagoueche, was built from 1698 at the mouth of the St John River (St John, New Brunswick) in the area of the previous forts Charmisay/La Tour/Martignon. It was abandoned following the end of the War of Spanish Succession in 1713. Disputes over the boundaries of Nova Scotia led Governor General de La Jonquière to dispatch a party of troops under the command of Captain Charles Deschamps de Boishébert from Canada to the area in 1750 with instructions to build a stockade fort with quarters for officers and 100 men on the spot. The new Fort Menagoueche (also spelt Fort Menacoche) was built and garrisoned with 20 soldiers and 50 Canadian militiamen. It was built of pine logs put up on a nearly square plan of 65 × 68 m (71 × 74 yd) with four bastions. Within were barracks, a storehouse, a powder magazine, and a well was dug. The buildings had stone foundations and were made of cedar timber covered with pine planks. There was neither a chapel nor missionary.

Fort Beauséjour (Aulac, New Brunswick) was built during 1751 to secure the frontier with British Nova Scotia. French troops, Canadian militiamen, and allied Indians had been sent from Canada since 1749 to secure the relatively vague border

Plan of Fort Beauséjour, 1751. This plan was probably drawn up by engineer Lieutenant Gaspard-Joseph de Léry in the fall of 1751 with its side notes forming a report on the progress of the fort's construction. The stockade wall consisted of two rows of logs planted in the ground. On the whole, progress was satisfying, and most planned structures were up except for the barracks (shown with the pale roof). The profile of the planned ditches and earthworks are shown at the top. Library and Archives Canada, MG 18, K5.

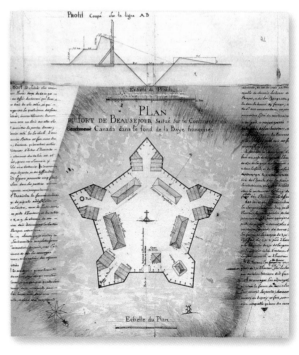

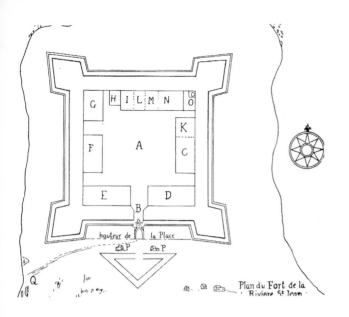

Plan of the Fort de la rivière Saint-Jean, October 20, 1700. The merchant Dièreville described this fort in 1699 as having earthen ramparts with four bastions, each mounted with six "large cannons." Its features were A: parade; B: gate; C: governor's residence; D: officers' lodgings; E: warehouse; F: barracks; G: powder magazine; H: jail; I: surgeon's quarters; M: armorer's quarters; L: gunners' quarters; O: well; P: ovens; Q: landing leading to the fort. The fort was originally built in 1645 on the west side of the present-day city of St John, New Brunswick. Private collection.

area from incursions by British troops. There were a number of tense moments between rival parties, especially in April 1750 when some 400 British troops led by Major Charles Lawrence wished to occupy Pointe Beauséjour and its hill, which they considered within British territory and the best place to build a fort. They found French troops already there. As Britain and France were not at war, there was no shooting, and the British built Fort Lawrence about 5 km (3.1 mi) to the south. In November 1750, Governor General de La Jonquière ordered that two forts, one large and one small, be built at each end of the Isthmus of Chignecto to block the British from going past it as well as to protect the Acadian settlement at Beaubassin. Fort Beauséjour was the large fort. It was situated on the height at Pointe Beauséjour facing Beaubassin (now Bassin Cumberland) and was laid out as a pentagon with five bastions built of earth and pickets with wooden buildings inside. Work started in April 1751 under the direction of the fort's designer, Engineer Lieutenant Gaspard-Joseph Chaussegros de Léry. During the summer, Chief Engineer Franquet came to the site and expanded on the plans to make the fort more secure against artillery fire, notably with wide earthen walls that featured an underground tunnel. Most of the fort was finished by the end of the year and its barracks finished in 1752.

Work also started during the spring of 1751 on building the smaller Fort Gaspareau at the northeastern end of the Isthmus of Chignecto at Baie Verte, about 30 km (18.6 mi) from Beauséjour. It had simple square plan of 37 m (40.5 yd) to a side with a tower at each corner. The walls consisted of a wooden stockade with a banquette and loophole, and the towers were made of squared timber. A ditch was dug around the fort. Barracks within the fort were planned but do not seem to have been built, its small garrison having adequate lodging in houses built outside the fort. This fort was built as a sentinel border station and not meant to sustain a regular siege.

The bloody incidents in the Ohio during 1754 resulted in the renewal of hostilities between Britain and France. Nova Scotia had the strongest garrison of the British seaboard colonies, and on June 2, 1755, some 2,000 British regular and Massachusetts provincial troops under Lieutenant Colonel Robert Monkton arrived at the Isthmus of Chigneto. After some skirmishes in the area, Fort Beauséjour was invested by the Anglo-American troops on June 12. From June 13–15, batteries bombarded the fort, which surrendered on June 16 and it was renamed Fort Cumberland. Fort Gaspareau was included in the capitulation. French commandant Duchambon de Vergor was later much criticized for what seemed a rather weak defense. However, his garrison consisted of only about 150 men with no hope of any relief force coming to his rescue from Canada. Following the fall of Fort Beauséjour, Fort Menagoueche was partly destroyed and abandoned by the French in July 1755. The French military threat on this frontier did not end with the fall of these forts. French and Indian groups, notably Acadian partisans, continued to wage guerrilla-style warfare in this area until they learned of the surrender of the French forces in Canada in late 1760.

PLAN et Profil du fort de Gaspareau Scitué Sur la Pte de Monsegu au fond de la Baye Verte faisant partie du Canada. 20° Aoust 1751

Profil de la Palissade double du fort avec le projet d'un fossé, et d'une Banquette

Following the cession of Acadia (Nova Scotia) and Placentia to Britain in 1713, the French did not maintain any substantial forts further to the west in the present province of New Brunswick. They did keep their influence with the allied Micmac Indians through missionaries, traders, and officers detached among them. Miramichi, on the north shore of Miramichi Bay, also had Acadian settlers. From 1756, Captain de Boishébert used it as a refuge for Acadians that had escaped the 1755 deportation from Nova Scotia and as a base for parties of Acadian partisans and Indians to harass the British. It featured a large settlement at Wilson's Point and a small fort on an island farther up the Miramichi River. Learning of the fall of Louisbourg, the Acadians and Indians evacuated the area in August 1758. The British destroyed the village in September 1758 and the fort on Boishébert Island in June 1760. Boishébert Island and nearby Wilson's Point now form Boishébert National Historic Site of Canada. However, another (seemingly unknown) post in the Miramichi area was occupied by a small detachment under Lieutenant de Niverville from the later part of 1760 until sometime in 1761.

From 1720, Isle Saint-Jean (now the Canadian province of Prince Edward Island) was settled by French Acadians. In 1726, a commandant with a small garrison was detached from Fortress Louisbourg; barracks, officers' quarters, and a powder magazine were built at Port La Joye (now Charlottetown). A fort was later proposed but never built. The island was occupied by Anglo-American troops after the fall of Louisbourg in 1745 but only after its small garrison and allied Indians had repulsed a first landing attempt before evacuating to Québec. Isle Saint-Jean was returned to France in 1748 and reoccupied in 1758, its 3,500 inhabitants deported.

Plaisance (Placentia)

French fishermen from Brittany are recorded in Newfoundland as early as 1504, but it was not until 1660 that a permanent settlement was attempted at Plaisance (renamed Placentia by the British) on the island's south coast. Little is known of this first failed attempt, save that it had a stockade fort armed with four cannons. Two years later, some settlers escorted by 30 soldiers landed to "replace" the initial group. This time, the settlement was successful, and another fort was built, apparently on the same site as the previous one. The new fort, made of earth and logs, was obviously larger as it had 18 guns in 1662–1663 and 32 in 1667. According to a plan from the 1670s, it had a polygonal layout with five small bastions. The colony was much neglected during most of the 1670s and 1680s and had no garrison; the fort consequently fell into disrepair.

A small regular garrison of colonial troops was posted in Placentia from 1687, but substantial fortifications were not built. On February 25, 1690, a strong party of English corsairs easily took Plaisance after a short fight and looted the place. A few reinforcements were sent in 1691, and the stockade Fort Louis with seven guns was put up in two weeks. During the following year, the Gaillardin redoubt was started on what is now the aptly named Castle Hill and a four-gun shore battery was built below. In September 1692, an English fleet bombarded Plaisance with roughly 2,000 cannonballs, but no landing was attempted. Improvements on the fortifications continued in the following years, notably by building a new redoubt on Castle Hill named Fort Royal. In late August 1693, British ships from the West Indies arrived off Placentia, they were quickly fired upon when they approached, and they sailed for England on September 3. The redoubt of Fort Royal was built on a square plan with four half bastions, its walls reveted with masonry. By 1701, Placentia was protected by Fort Louis near the shore with many adjoining small shore

ABOVE
The first French fort at Plaisance (now Placentia, Newfoundland) in the 1660s. According to this illustration, it was built on a polygonal plan with five bastions. It is shown much larger than it really was and did not occupy as much space. The forts built in the 1690s did not use this site. Fort Louis was built on the point marked "Grave" facing the narrow channel (bottom center of plan). The masonry Fort Royal was built on top of Castle Hill (bottom left) along with the Guillardin redoubt. Library and Archives Canada.

RIGHT
Fort Royal, Plaisance, 1695. This plan and elevation shows the square fort with half bastions built on top of what later became known as Castle Hill, a commanding height that overlooks the town of Placentia. The wooden board platforms were set on packed earth. In addition to the fort's small square parade, there was a three-room barracks (bottom), a guardhouse and storehouse on either side of the gate (top), and at the center, a square blockhouse with a plank platform on its roof. The fort had masonry walls, and the blockhouse may also have had stone walls. The blockhouse had been removed by 1701 and a second story and pitched roof added to the barracks. Library and Archives Canada.

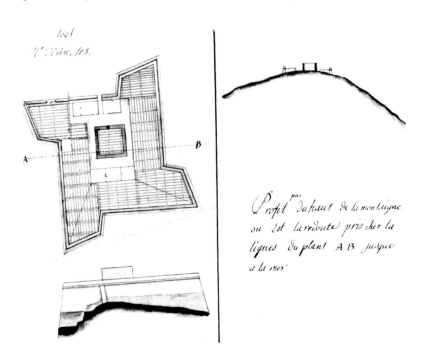

batteries, and the stone-built Fort Royal on top of Castle Hill with its nearby wooden Gaillardin redoubt. In March 1703, Placentia was blockaded by British ships, but these soon departed. Placentia was the base for French raids made by land onto the British settlements in Newfoundland. These raids were, on the whole, quite successful, and even St. John's was taken in 1709, an action that basically expelled the British from Newfoundland. They kept up a fairly effective blockade on the French in Placentia until the Treaty of Utrecht was signed in 1713. In that treaty, all of Newfoundland, including Placentia, was ceded to Great Britain. It signalled the end of the French presence in Newfoundland, and Placentia's garrison and many of its inhabitants moved to Cape Breton Island.

St Lawrence River Valley

From the Gulf of the St Lawrence River to Québec City, settlements were few and far between. The area leading north and through the Strait of Belle-Isle and toward Labrador was dotted with a few trading posts, some dating back to seasonal stations kept by Basque fishermen during the 16th and early 17th centuries, such as Baie Forteau or Baie Rouge (now Red Bay, Labrador). The Inuit natives often drove the traders and fishermen away to loot the posts as happened, for instance, to the Baie Rouge fort that was destroyed by them

in 1719 and rebuilt by French traders in 1721. No troops were posted in that area. The Gulf of St Lawrence had a few trade forts, as did the great fur trade area up the Saguenay River to Lake Saint-Jean, with posts such as Chicoutimi and Métabéchouan. There might be small posts and lookout stations on the shores going west, but it was only at Québec City that very substantial military fortifications worthy of one of the great fortresses in America were seen. There were no substantial military fortifications with regular garrisons between Québec and Trois-Rivières until the last year of the French Regime.

Following the Battle of the Plains and the loss of Québec to the British in September 1759, General Lévis ordered a substantial field fortification named Fort Jacques-Cartier built on the shores of the Jacques-Cartier River at Cap-Santé, west of the city. This post blocked British troops from going farther west and also served as a logistical base when Lévis tried to besiege Québec in April and May 1760. The arrival of British reinforcements frustrated Lévis's attempt, but Fort Jacques-Cartier

Madeleine de Verchères at the seigneurial fort of Verchères on October 22, 1692. Suddenly attacked by a band of Iroquois, Madeleine ran to her fort and "having reached the gates at last, I found there two women lamenting for the loss of their husbands, who had just been killed. I made them enter the fort, and closed the gates myself." After convincing two soldiers named La Bonté and Galhet not to blow themselves up in the powder magazine, this 14-year-old daughter of the seigneur de Verchères conducted a shrewd and successful defense for a week, until troops came to her relief. This plate by C. W. Jefferys gives a fair impression of the interior of a seigneurial fort. Private collection.

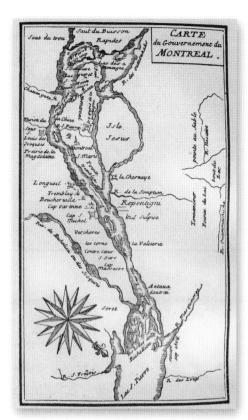

remained the forward bastion of the French Army until late summer 1760. In August, General James Murray's army marched past the fort on its way to Montréal. After Montréal's surrender on September 8, Fort Jacques-Cartier with its garrison of 50 French regulars and 150 Canadian militiamen under Lieutenant d'Alberghetti still held out. On September 10, a force of some 700 British troops under Colonel Fraser arrived, and, after an exchange of musket fire, the fort's garrison finally surrendered. A small British garrison was posted there until 1763, the place then being abandoned. It has since remained relatively untouched, and, following archeological work carried out during the 1960s, it has been the subject of preservation efforts as the features of its field fortifications are still largely perceptible on the site.

From the early 1670s when many seigneuries were granted in the St Lawrence River Valley, mostly to former officers of the Carignan-Salières Regiment, a number of seigneurial forts were built, sometimes with the help of soldiers, to provide protection for the settlers in case of an attack by marauding bands of Iroquois. This was especially the case in the Montréal area. Those forts closest to the city that formed an integral part of its defenses are covered in *French Fortresses in North America 1535–1763* (Osprey Fortress 27). Other forts were built in seigneuries farther east up to the Trois-Rivières area beyond which the menace was not as acute. In the late 1680s, with a renewal of the war with the Iroquois, more seigneurial forts were built. Squads of soldiers were detached to help garrison some of them. The two forts described below were among the more notable.

Map of the Montréal "Government," or District, c. 1670. The orientation is west at top, east at bottom, north at right, and south at left. Only a few forts are shown, but in fact nearly all localities had some sort of fort built by the local "seigneur" such as the famous one at Verchères. Private collection.

Fort Verchères, about 50 km (31 mi) east of Montréal, was probably typical of these seigneurial forts. It had a 15-ft-high stockade with bastions on a square plan that enclosed the seigneur's house, barns, stables, and a redoubt that served as a guardhouse and magazine. The side with the gate faced the St Lawrence River, and a 10-ft-wide moat surrounded the three other sides. The fort, which had a cannon, was big enough to give refuge to

A fort "like so many built by the French" in Canada and especially typical of the seigneurial stockade enclosures built from the 1670s in the St Lawrence River Valley between Montréal and Trois-Rivières, often with the church and seigneur's house within. Most of these forts appear to have been built on a square plan with bastions, as shown in this late-19th-century print. Private collection.

the settlers and their cattle. In 1690, an Iroquois raid was repulsed by the seigneuress de Verchères, but it was her 14-year-old daughter, Madeleine, who gained lasting fame in Canadian history books for her extraordinary stand against a band of Iroquois from October 22–30, 1692, with her two young brothers, her servant, two soldiers, an old man of 80, and some frightened women and children.

Built in 1687, Fort Crevier, also known as Fort Saint-François, was a wooden structure built by Jean Crevier, the seigneur of Saint-François, on the south shore of the St Lawrence, at the mouth of the Saint-François River. Several skirmishes between the Iroquois and the French occurred nearby, although the fort itself was not attacked. In November 1689, several inhabitants were killed and the newly built chapel was burned. In another raid during August 1693, Crevier was captured by the Iroquois; they planned to torture him to death, but he was bought and freed by Captain Peter Schuyler of Albany, although Crevier is said to have died from his wounds shortly thereafter. In August 1700, part of the seigneury was ceded to the allied Abenakis Indians to create the mission of Saint-François, better known to Americans as St Francis. The fort itself seems to have been abandoned following the end of hostilities with the Iroquois in 1701.

This was the fate of dozens of seigneurial forts in the 18th century. In 1729–1730, fears of renewed warfare led Governor General de Beauharnois to send an engineer to have the forts repaired and their walls rebuilt with stone. But there was no real need anymore for such forts. Twenty years later, when Colonel Franquet made his inspection tour, most had vanished.

The Richelieu River and Lake Champlain Valley
Forts of the Richelieu River
Named in honor of Cardinal Richelieu, France's outstanding prime minister in the early 17th century, the Richelieu River has its source in Lake Champlain and flows north into the St Lawrence River. It was one of the first rivers to be explored by the French, and in, 1609, Champlain, accompanied by bands of allied Indians, went south as far as the area of Ticonderoga. There, on July 30, Champlain came upon the Iroquois Indians, enemies of his allied Indians; they were routed because he was wearing armor and because he fired a harquebus, killing a couple of their chiefs. The Iroquois were not about to let the French forget this action, and it heralded nearly a century of hostilities. The Richelieu River had always been the Indians' north–south highway, and the French soon learned to nickname it the *"rivière des Iroquois"* (the Iroquois' river). It was the main waterway north for the Mohawk raiding parties that then wandered up the St Lawrence.

Before 1642, the French only had settlements at Québec and Trois-Rivières (from 1634), the latter often being targeted by the marauding Iroquois. With the 1642 foundation of a new settlement on the island of Montréal, situated

Fort Jacques-Cartier, 1759–1760. Built in September 1759, this fort built west of Québec City at Cap-Santé surrendered on September 10, 1760. It was built as an earthen and wooden field fortification on the west side of the Jacques-Cartier River to be a redoubt facing the St Lawrence. It also featured a long inland spur going north that cut off and controlled the King's Highway between Montréal and Québec at its ford at the Jacques-Cartier River. Plan after Sieur de Courville. Private collection.

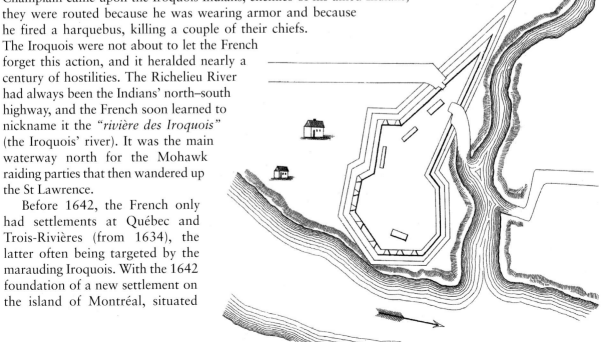

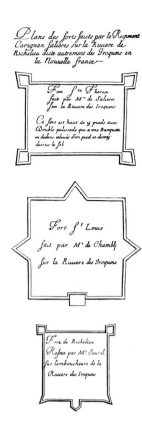

some 90 km (56 mi) west of the Richelieu meeting the St Lawrence, the problem of the Iroquois coming up from the south had to be addressed. Fort Richelieu (now Sorel, QC), a stockade work, was built at the mouth of the river during August 1642 to block the Iroquois. The fort contained a chapel and lodgings for its small garrison of about one dozen soldiers. Allied Indians settled nearby but were eventually driven away by marauding Iroquois. While the fort was a hindrance, the Iroquois bypassed it by land, and in late 1644, resolved to blockade it. There were countless skirmishes until the fort was abandoned, probably in early 1647, and burned by the Iroquois in February of that year. Such was the fate of the first fort in the Richelieu Valley.

In the early 1660s, young King Louis XIV was given alarming reports concerning his fledgling colony of Canada. The settlers were on the verge of being overcome by the "barbarian nation of the Iroquois" to quote the king's memoirs. This was certainly not to be tolerated in the realm of the new Sun King, and in summer 1665, some 1,200 regular soldiers, mostly belonging to the Carignan-Salières Regiment, were detached from the French metropolitan army and landed at Québec. They were to secure the colony against the Iroquois and then attack them. Finally, all officers and soldiers who wished to remain in Canada as settlers would be encouraged to stay. The new governor general, the Marquis de Tracy, directed that three forts would be built on the shores of the Richelieu River. The first one was built by Captain Pierre de Saurel and his men from July 23 to October 15 on the site of the abandoned Fort Richelieu. They erected a wooden work that was 100 ft square with four bastions; it became known as Fort Sorel. The second fort, named St Louis, was built farther downriver by Captain Jacques de Chambly and his men, and became commonly known as Fort Chambly. The third fort was situated about a kilometre north of Fort Chambly, and named Fort Sainte-Thérèse. It was a rectangular stockade with a small bastion at each corner and was constructed in September 1665. It was realized that more forts were needed to close the river to the Iroquois. The following August, Fort l'Assomption was built below Fort Chambly and became better known as Fort Saint-Jean and Fort Sainte-Anne on the north end of Lake Champlain.

Using the Richelieu forts as bases, the French troops went into Iroquois territory during 1666; the enemy Indians were not destroyed, but they were certainly overawed. During 1667, a peace treaty was concluded between the French governor and the Iroquois. The troops either became settlers in Canada

Interior of Fort Chambly. The chapel roof is restored according to its appearance as rebuilt in 1750. The marks on the ground of the center courtyard indicate features of the 1702 fort found during archeological work. At lower right, a line of logs from the stockade and buildings at the center.

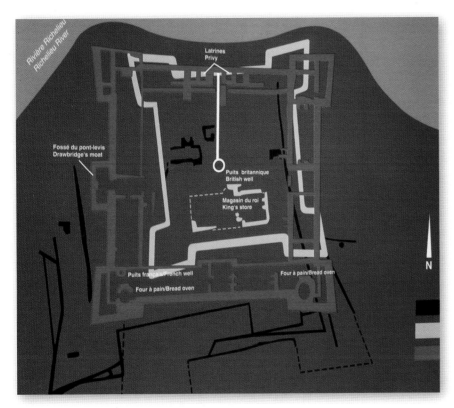

Fort Chambly ground plans, 1665 to today. This site actually holds the outlines for three successive forts built there. The lines in black show the features associated with the first fort built in 1665. The archeologist uncovered half bastions on the landward south side, which indicate it had major modifications from its original plan at an undetermined date, and certainly again later, probably in 1693. The second fort built in 1702 is indicated by the outline in beige. The third and present fort, built in stone from 1709, is indicated by the red outline. The round central circle and its underground canal indicated in white is a well that was later added by the British. Fort Chambly National Historic Site, Chambly, Québec.

or were gradually sent back to France during 1667 and 1668, except for two companies left in Montréal and two at Fort Chambly that provided detachments to forts Saint-Jean and Sainte-Anne. With the disbandment of these companies in 1671, the regular garrison of Canada only amounted to an establishment of 67 for the three towns of Québec, Trois-Rivières, and Montréal, including 20

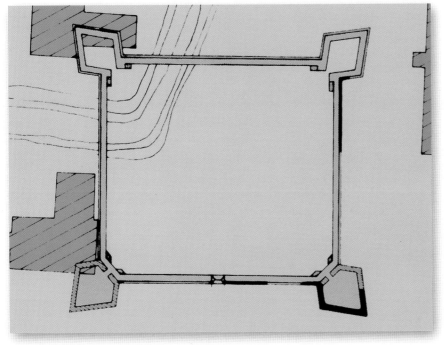

Outline of Fort Saint-Jean built in 1748 as a supply base, according to trial excavations by Parks Canada archeologist Gisèle Piédalue in the 1980s. Features in black were uncovered, and the perimeter in brown largely determined. The east bastions (bottom) facing the Richelieu River were closed buildings while the west bastions were open. The lines at upper left are features associated with the later British fortifications built there, and the darkly shaded squares are present structures associated with the Collège Militaire Royal that was closed by the government in the mid 1990s. Parks Canada.

guards for the governor general. The Richelieu river forts were thus abandoned except for two, forts Chambly and Sorel. While they do not seem to have had garrisons for nearly two decades after, both forts had growing settlements next to them and were kept up by militiamen and traders.

Renewed warfare with the Iroquois broke out in the early 1680s, and from 1683, troops were sent to permanently garrison Canada. By 1686–1687, soldiers were back in forts Chambly and Sorel, but their fortifications were found to be in poor shape, as parts of their stockades had rotted. The walls of both forts were rebuilt and the interior buildings repaired during 1693. Parties of Iroquois lurked everywhere along the Richelieu and east of Montréal during the 1680s and 1690s. The number of small engagements between the Iroquois and the French were countless. In 1696 for instance, a band of Iroquois looted and set some houses on fire outside the fort at Sorel. However, it was an accidental fire that totally destroyed Fort Chambly in 1702. As this was the only fort on the Richelieu River, another stockade, Fort Chambly, was immediately built that year. It had a rectangular plan with bastions and two large buildings inside.

Meanwhile, French troops and Canadian militiamen had penetrated deep into the Iroquois' homelands during the 1690s. Thanks to a combination of Indian tactics and European discipline as well as skillful diplomacy with native nations, the French in Canada gradually vanquished the Iroquois during the 1690s. By 1700, the natives were on the defensive and suffering from famine. In a master diplomatic stroke, the French concluded the Great Peace of Montréal in 1701, an assembly that gathered Iroquois as well as delegates from allied Indian nations from as far as the western Great Lakes. This peace, which largely neutralized the Iroquois while ensuring a web of alliances with western Indians, held until the late 1750s.

While the Iroquois menace was now contained, a much greater challenged loomed. The Anglo-American colonies to the south were growing rapidly in population, prosperity, and strength. From 1690, the colonies had even raised substantial forces aimed at the conquest of Canada. All attempts had failed, but the occasional gathering of thousands of New England militiamen south of Lake Champlain was a growing concern to the military authorities in New France. Raids by New York militiamen and allied Mohawks had penetrated as far as Laprairie, south of Montréal, in 1691; they had been repulsed with loss, but this had shown just how far such a force could get. During Queen Anne's War (1702–1713), New Englanders mustered again, causing concern in Québec that an invasion of Canada was imminent. The only possible invasion route into Canada by land was for an army to go up by the Richelieu River, an area guarded only by the stockade walls of Fort Chambly. The threat of an Anglo-American invasion became increasingly serious so that, in 1709, Governor General Vaudreuil ordered the construction of a substantial masonry fort at Chambly.

Fort Sorel (or Richelieu) in 1666. This stockade fort was built in 1665, apparently on the site of the 1642–1647 Fort Richelieu. It was situated on the east bank of the Richelieu River (top) at its meeting with the St Lawrence River (right). The east side featured two full bastions shown here much larger than on the 1665 plan of Richelieu River forts. It was surrounded by a wide ditch. Its walls featured two rows of musket loopholes. Fort Sorel was rebuilt in stone during the early 18th century. Print after an original plan. Private collection.

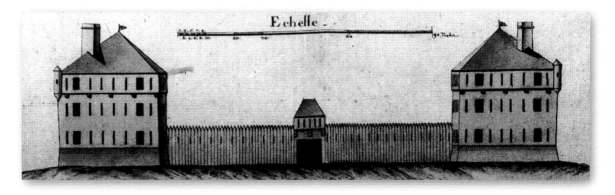

Chief Engineer Josué Boisberthelot de Beaucours conceived a structure that would resist an attack by an army equipped with small-caliber artillery. At that time, it was considered extremely unlikely that batteries of heavy siege artillery could be brought from the upper Hudson River, in the colony of New York, to the Richelieu River. This third Fort Chambly was thus to be radically different from its predecessors, not only because it was made of stone but also because of its novel design. Instead of the low Vauban-style walls and bastions usually seen in Europe, the new Fort Chambly was built during 1710–1711 on a square plan featuring curtain walls that were nearly 10 m (32.8 ft) high and 1 m (3.3 ft) thick. The bastions at each corner were designed to be high, squared turrets. The walls and turrets were pierced with numerous embrasures. The fort's only gate was on its north side. It was an imposing structure reminiscent of medieval castles and meant to impress, especially the Indians, as well as to provide defense for the colony.

Amazingly, this type of fort did in fact follow Marshal Vauban's instructions. In 1699, when reviewing the type of fortifications made in Canada, he commented to the minister of the Navy that "there could be no question" of building fortifications there as in Europe. He recommended instead that colonial fortifications consist of "well-enclosed areas" that should have stone walls "with towers like those of small towns or large villages [in France] or earthen entrenchments with [wooden] palisades." In effect, this was a sort of updated medieval-style castle, which is exactly what Chief Engineer de Beaucours had built at Chambly. He undoubtedly was aware of Marshal Vauban's recommendation, as was his successor. When finished, Fort Chambly was capable of housing a garrison of up to 500 men and could be armed with up to 40 cannons and 36 swivel guns in an emergency. As it turned out, the Anglo-American invasion plans of 1709 and 1711 were not implemented, and in 1713 the Treaty of Utrecht ended hostilities.

Canada now had a substantial fort to guard the Richelieu River invasion route. Indeed, Fort Chambly was considered by Governor General Vaudreuil to be "the most useful" fortification ever built in the colony. It had been built only a few years when the new chief engineer, Gaspard Chaussegros de Léry (who held the post from 1716 to 1756), had major changes and improvements made between 1718 and 1720. Fort Chambly remained the main defense for the southern access to Canada until the 1730s when it was decided to build fortifications farther south. Thereafter, it lost its strategic importance but remained a garrisoned logistical base for men and supplies moving up and down the river. In 1753, Colonel Louis Franquet, on an engineering inspection tour, strongly and correctly argued that Fort Chambly was an essential link in Canada's defense.

Fort Saint-Jean on the Richelieu River in 1750. The second Fort Saint-Jean was built as a large supply depot. It featured the large tower bastions and palisades typical of many Canadian forts. Library and Archives Canada.

Fort Chambly, 1718–1740s

The stone-built Fort Chambly was constructed in 1710–1711. It had high turret-like bastions and high curtain walls against which the inside buildings were erected. From 1718 to 1720, the fort underwent major transformations aimed at improving its defensive capacity. The curtain wall facing the water was rebuilt and pierced with six vaulted cannon emplacements with embrasures. A small gate with a small machicolation above was situated in the middle of this wall. Wooden *guérites* – the small lookout sentry boxes – were added at the top corner of each bastion. On the west wall, the main gate's safety was much improved by the addition of a machicolation above it, a drawbridge, and a ditch. While not intended to sustain a long siege but rather to have the capacity to repulse an assault by a sizable force, the stone castle-like Fort Chambly certainly made an impressive first stop for anyone coming up the Richelieu River into Canada. With the construction of Fort Saint-Frédéric farther south during the 1730s, Fort Chambly's importance declined, and it became more of a depot for troops and supplies on the way south. The vaulted batteries in the north curtain walls had been turned into warehouses by 1744, when the six 4-pdr cannons were sent to Fort Saint-Frédéric, but could be easily rearmed as shown in plans dated 1750. At that time, some second-story gables were removed, and the roof of the chapel at the south curtain wall was rebuilt. The restorations undertaken at Fort Chambly in the 1980s have more or less recreated its appearance during the 1750s.

Although not as strategically important as Chambly, Fort Sorel was rebuilt in stone during the second quarter of the 18th century on a square plan with four bastions. By then, this post was a mixture of military and civilian features. Within its walls were the seigneur's residence, a small church and the priest's house (until 1734 when a new church was built outside), a guardhouse for the soldiers, a stable, and a stone windmill with a small house for the miller. Nearby was a thriving community of about 600 souls.

As the supply route became longer – reaching the southern tip of Lake Champlain, notably thanks to a 45-ton vessel – the Richelieu River gained in logistical importance to the point that, during the 1740s, the need for another fort became apparent. In 1747, a stockade was built on the site of the old 1665 Fort Sainte-Thérèse to act as a fortified supply depot. A road had been built to send supplies by wagon between Laprairie and Saint-Jean so that, in 1748, another Fort Saint-Jean was built on the spot of the 1665–1671 fort bearing the same name, and the Sainte-Thérèse depot was dismantled. The new Fort Saint-Jean was designed on a square plan as a fortified warehouse enclosure; there was no doubt it could not resist a strong force equipped with artillery. It had wooden palisades connecting to bastions with stone foundations 6 ft above the ground, the two bastions facing the river being of squared timber three stories high to lodge the garrison and its supplies.

Lake Champlain Valley
Explored by Champlain as early as 1609, the Lake Champlain Valley became a pressing strategic concern for the French in Canada in the first part of the 18th century. Following an alarming dispatch by Captain Lacorne de Saint-Luc in 1730, Governor General de Beauharnois resolved to build a small fort at Pointe-à-la-chevelure at the southern end of Lake Champlain – a place known as Crown Point by the British. If the Anglo-Americans were to build a fort there, it would provide them with an ideal base to move an army toward Canada. In summer 1731, troops moved down to the site and built Fort Pointe-à-la-chevelure, a small stockade fort of about 50 ft square with bastions, which was finished by September 29 and provided with a small garrison of regular colonial troops of 20 men.

The gate at the stone-built Fort Chambly erected from 1720 with the *machicoulis* over the doorway. The royal coat of arms would have been added around 1725 when forts, cities, and public buildings were directed to put up this insignia over their gates. Various names were engraved on the stones in the late 19th century. This gate was refurbished in the 1980s as part of the extensive restoration of the fort by Parks Canada.

Fort Saint-Frédéric, 1740. This view, drawn only three years after the fort's construction ended, also shows the windmill built just outside in 1738. The Reverend John Norton, captured at the surrender of Fort Massachusetts, described the fort as he saw it on August 28, 1746: "It is something of an irregular form having five sides to it; the ramparts twenty feet thick, the breastwork two feet and a half; the whole about twenty feet high. There were twenty-one or twenty-two guns upon the wall; some four and six pounders and there may be some as large as nine pounders. The citadel is octagon built, three stories high, fifty or sixty feet diameter, built with stone laid in lime, the wall six or seven feet thick, arched over the second and third stories for bomb proof. In the chambers nine or ten guns; some of them may be nine pounders, and I believe none less than six, and near twenty patararoes [guns]. But as my time [there] was short, I cannot be very particular." Detail from a map. Library of Congress, Washington, DC.

This was only a first effort. As the Anglo-Americans were not very far away and would easily overcome this small fort in the event of a war, Chief Engineer Chassegros de Léry was sent to the site in 1731 to draft plans for a much stronger masonry work. What he proposed was a large redoubt in the form of a towerlike structure four stories high with a machicolation above and a high roof. This lay at the northeast corner of a square masonry enclosure with bastions and curtain walls pierced with musket loopholes and ordnance embrasures. The design may have seemed unusual to European eyes, but it followed the recommendations of Marshal Vauban for forts in Canada. Like Fort Chambly, it was meant to counter an assault and not a prolonged siege by an enemy equipped with heavy ordnance. After some hesitation in Versailles, approval was given in 1734 by the minister of the Navy to build this masonry fort.

Construction started in 1735 and went on for several years. By fall 1737, the redoubt and walls were completed, but ordnance had not arrived. The following year, a windmill was built just outside the fort and six iron 4-pdrs and six swivel guns were installed; six more iron 4-pdrs were sent from Fort Chambly in 1744. From 1738, the Fort Pointe-à-la-chevelure changed its name to Fort Saint-Frédéric, taken from one of the names of the minister of the Navy, Jean-Frédéric Count de Maurepas. The usual garrison was of 100 men in summer and 50 men in winter, figures that fluctuated greatly during the War of Austrian Succession (1744–1748). During that war, Fort Saint-Frédéric was the base for large French and Indian raiding parties. The Anglo-Americans also intended to attack Fort Saint-Frédéric, but nothing came of their plans. Instead, the French raiding parties took and burned the stockade Fort Lydius in 1745, where the portages from the Hudson River to Lake George were made, leaving practically no British defenses north of Albany.

Imposing as it looked to colonial Americans and Indians, Fort Saint-Frédéric appears not to have impressed most French officers who later saw it. In the 1750s, generals Montcalm and Lévis as well as Bougainville, De la Pause, and artillery commander Le Mercier all agreed that is was a "bad fort" that was poorly situated and within range of commanding heights. Time had passed, and the notion of large armies moving through the wilderness with heavy artillery was a distinct possibility by the middle of the 1750s. The fortifications of Fort Saint-Frédéric had thus become redundant.

Ticonderoga

In spring 1755, hostilities had not yet been formally declared between France and Britain, but a state of war already existed following battles between French and Anglo-American troops in the contested Ohio Valley. With an outdated Fort Saint-Frédéric to guard its southern access to Canada, a new fort was urgently needed to guard the vital Lake Champlain and Richelieu River waterways. Both countries sent metropolitan troops to reinforce their respective domains. The British under General Edward Braddock were vanquished by French colonial troops, Canadian militiamen, and allied Indians near Fort Duquesne in July 1755. The French troops under Baron Dieskau went down past Lake Champlain to be repulsed by American militiamen at Lake George in early September. Both metropolitan generals

An evocative profile of Fort Saint-Frédéric as it appeared from 1737 to 1759, set on a glass plate that overlays the archeological ruins of the fort in the distance. Just beyond the fort, out of focus, is the modern bridge linking the states of New York and Vermont. This plate can be seen in the interpretation center maintained by the State of New York at Crown Point State Historic Site.

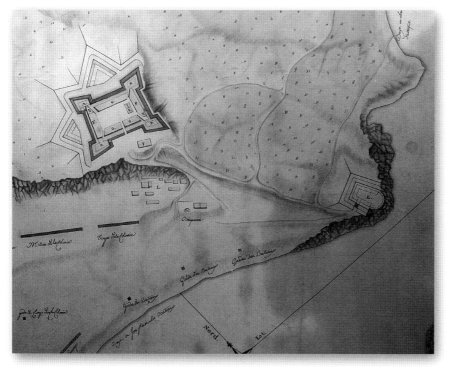

Plan of the peninsula at Ticonderoga, summer 1756. Fort Carillon is situated on a bluff; note its interior buildings with slanted walls to provide increased space. Below the fort lie a number of buildings including a place to make bricks. Regular troops, Canadian militia, and Indians were encamped between the buildings and the boat landing. Plan by Captain Germain of the La Reine Regiment, detached as acting engineer. Fort Ticonderoga Museum.

Fort Saint-Frédéric (Crown Point), 1738–1759

The French first built a small fort at the southern end of Lake Champlain during 1731 while planning a much larger masonry work completed by 1737–1738. Its main features were a large tower four stories high that served as a redoubt and lodging for the garrison. It was designed to impress the Anglo-Americans and Indians, and it certainly did; they had nothing like it on their side of the wilderness frontier. The tower lay within a stone wall built on a square plan with bastions at the corners. The wall had loopholes and gun ports for artillery that could easily repulse any raiding party or small force. It was not designed to withstand a siege by a large enemy army provided with an artillery train – an extremely unlikely possibility during the first two decades after it was built.

An early bird's-eye view of Fort Carillon at Ticonderoga, NY, taken in the 1920s. This colored photograph shows the fort before most its reconstruction, notably the stabilized foundations of buildings on the south and east sides. The slanting side walls of the buildings are clearly visible. Private collection.

The Lotbinière Battery at Ticonderoga, 1756–1759. Although Fort Carillon controlled the junction of Lakes Champlain and Saint-Sacrement (Lake George), a rocky bluff obstructed the view on the connecting river to the east. By hugging the shore, enemy boats might pass undetected. To correct this, the Lotbinière battery was built during 1756–1757 to command any movement on the river. A covered way connected the battery to Fort Carillon. Model by Roger Duchame, Fort Ticonderoga Museum.

were lost, and it was an inauspicious start. The new governor general of New France, the Canadian-born Marquis de Vaudreuil – his father had been governor general from 1701 to 1725 – had just assumed office. Seeing the gaping hole created by Baron Dieskau's defeat in the southern sector, he immediately gave instructions to build a substantial masonry fort south of Fort Saint-Frédéric, at Ticonderoga, just above the northern end of Lake George (known as Saint-Sacrement by the French).

A young Canadian engineer, Michel Chartier de Lotbinière, was sent down to the area in fall 1755. He selected a site overlooking the narrow entrance of Wood Creek into the La Chute River connecting Lake George to Lake Champlain. It was east of a series of turbulent rapids whose sound inspired the French to call the area "Carillon" because it reminded them of church bells. Ticonderoga was the name used by the Indians and the Anglo-Americans to denote the place. As early as mid-October, work began on Fort Carillon, a standard European-style fort designed on a square plan with large bastions, ditches, ravelins, and glacis. Progress was swift, with 650 men of the La Reine and Languedoc regiments providing labor; by December, the fort's outline with temporary barracks and huts inside was already in place, and work on the walls was starting. The initial walls had a 10-ft-wide masonry foundation, above which a revetment of squared, heavy oak timbers was laid one on top of another on the outer and inner sides, and the center filled with earth and rubble. This was faster to build than masonry, and with the British said to be in the area, it was important to put up the fort quickly. Ordnance was also sent down, and by February 1756, 12 cannons were mounted and more were on the way. Thereafter, with the troops campaigning, work was slower, but by mid-July, the bastions were up to at least 7 ft high. By the end of the year some 36 cannons were mounted, a dozen of them heavy 16-pdrs.

When De Lotbinière had selected the site in 1755, the peninsula was nearly completely covered with trees and brush. Less than a year later, it was all but denuded, revealing that the fort was too far from the narrows to the east for effective artillery fire; a redoubt was built farther east to cover this area. A cluster of log buildings protected by a stockade was also situated between the fort and the river. The most notable was a large storehouse with cannons mounted on its roof that acted as a rectangular ravelin in front of the fort's gate. A large garden lay to the east of the fort.

In summer 1757, Major General Louis-Joseph Marquis de Montcalm's army went from Ticonderoga to besiege and take the British Fort William-Henry at the lower end of Lake George. That year, work started on replacing the fort's log revetments with masonry. The following year, over 17,000 troops led by Major General James Abercromby, the largest Anglo-American army ever seen in North America, headed toward Ticonderoga. On July 8, Abercromby's army attacked Montcalm's 4,200 French troops, entrenched in fieldworks west of Fort Carillon, the French roundly defeated the Anglo-American troops. As such, Fort Carillon did not play a big part in the battle of Ticonderoga as the enemy never came close to its walls. The only notable event was when its guns in the southwest bastions opened up on British barges approaching on La Chute River, sinking a couple of them. Nevertheless, the fort's strategic importance was vital; had Montcalm and his army been defeated that day, it is likely that Canada's resistance might have collapsed in the following months.

The British were not discouraged and redoubled their efforts in 1759. While Montcalm faced Major General James Wolfe at the siege of Québec, where both would be killed in September, another Anglo-American army was moving on Lake Ontario, and Major General Jeffery Amherst's 11,000 men headed toward Ticonderoga. This time, there were not enough troops in Canada to properly garrison all fronts. The defense perimeter was henceforth restrained to the St Lawrence and Richelieu valleys. The vital strategic importance of fortifications farther south thus collapsed, and they suddenly became expendable outposts. Forts Carillon and Saint-Frédéric were left with a few hundred men under Colonel François-Charles de Bourlamaque, with instructions to delay the British as best they could, then blow up the forts and retreat to Canada. By 1759, Fort Carillon's walls were approximately half-covered with masonry, and the place had been constantly worked on; British engineers considered it stronger than the previous year. Abercromby had attacked immediately without his artillery or reliable intelligence. Amherst, on the contrary, was very careful and methodical. By July 23, 1759, his large army had started siege operations, and three days later, the 400-man French garrison withdrew, blowing up the fort's powder magazine as they did so. On August 31, Bourlamaque evacuated his troops from Fort Saint-Frédéric, which was also blown up. The French troops, about 2,500 strong, headed north to a new position on Isle-aux-Noix in the Richelieu River. Amherst could not follow; the French had four vessels on Lake Champlain, and he had none. The conquest of Canada would have to wait until he could build a superior fleet, and work soon started on doing just that.

Isle-aux-Noix

All that now stood between Lake Champlain and Montréal were the inadequate warehouse forts at Saint-Jean, Chambly, and Sorel. Foreseeing this, a new work had been built from May on the southern end of Isle-aux-Noix to slow down and perhaps even halt invaders coming up Lake Champlain. The island's position in the middle of the Richelieu River made it possible to control all river traffic; with the west channel about 350 m (382 yd) wide and the eastern one about 230 m (251 yd) wide, they could easily be commanded by artillery batteries. The island itself was over 1,350 m (.83 mi) long by about 400 m (437 yd) in width. Before the start of the fortification work, it was nearly all covered by walnut trees, hence its name; a year later, few trees were left.

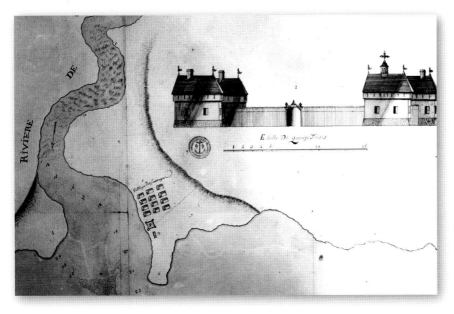

Fort La Présentation, 1752. In the upper right, a profile view of the fort with its massive yet elegant-looking tower bastions connected by a palisade. English prisoner Peter Williamson described it as "made of stockades with four block-houses, one in each corner, mounted with a few small swivel guns." At left, a site plan of the fort and the Indian village laid out in a neat square grid in rows. The Oswegatchie River, coming from the top of the picture, flows into the St Lawrence. Library and Archives Canada, C16239.

Fort Carillon, 1758–1759

Fort Carillon, now better known as Fort Ticonderoga, was designed with large bastions, ditches, ravelins, and glacis. Work started in the fall of 1755, and the fort went up quickly. Many guns were sent to arm the fort, some three dozen being mounted on its walls by the middle of 1756. It was planned as a masonry fort, but wood was used extensively. The walls had a 10-ft wide masonry foundation, on top of which squared heavy oak timbers were laid and the center filled with earth and rubble. In 1757, work went on to replace the rampart's timber revetment with stone, but it is uncertain how much was actually done. The ravelins and the buildings inside the fort were built of stone, but the curtain walls and the bastions were built of timber laid on a foundation of stone, providing a level surface upon which to build. Embrasures all around were made of wood, making parapets obviously wider than they are in the reconstructed stone fort. There was a building on the north side, but almost nothing is known about it, and there is nothing to indicate what it looked like. There is very little mention of it in period correspondence and plans, and only a couple old photographs show the ruins of some stonework in that area. This building has been omitted from this reconstruction.

Engineer François Fournier, newly arrived in Canada, was given the task of starting the work. In 1760, Michel Chartier de Lotbinière became the engineer in charge. Earthen entrenchments on the island's flat topography were really the only option, and Fournier designed an irregular enclosure punctuated with redans on its southern part with a hornwork on the northern side. The parapet was about 8 ft high with a banquette inside and a moat about 8 ft deep and 18 ft wide. Trees and branches were used for a fraise in the middle of the parapet and a berm in the moat. In 1760, de Lotbinière added the second line of entrenchment at the center of the island, two redoubts and a blockhouse. The ordnance within amounted to about 63 cannons, but only three heavy caliber 16-pdrs and 14 iron swivel guns. The five plans and sketches showing

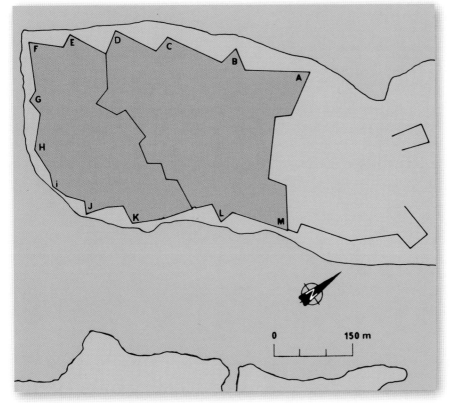

0   150 m

Outline of the fortifications of Fort Isle-aux-Noix in 1759–1760 as determined by Parks Canada historian André Charbonneau. None of the contemporary plans are totally accurate, and some even show structures that were never actually built. This island site was subject to extensive archeological excavation and research from the 1960s to the 1980s to determine the structural history of the various forts built on top of one another from 1759 onwards. Fort Lennox, dating from 1826, is the fort visible today and is arguably one of the most pristine National Historic sites in the northeast. Parks Canada.

these works disagree on various aspects, all showing features that were never constructed. After considerable research, historian André Charbonneau has determined the most likely trace for the various entrenchments on the island. It was reckoned that a garrison of up to 3,000 men was required to hold this large fortification, which had a perimeter of about 2,000 m (1.2 mi) including 400 m (437 yd) facing the hornwork.

By August 1760, the British had a lake fleet that dwarfed the few French vessels. In mid-August, a British vanguard came up the Richelieu and landed on the east bank facing Isle-aux-Noix, followed by about 3,000 men under Brigadier General William Haviland with 40 guns. Batteries were set up, and the siege started on August 16. The French could muster only about 1,450 men led by Colonel Louis-Antoine, Comte de Bougainville, and, after the loss of Québec, the lack of vital supplies and the feeling that it would soon be all over, meant that morale was relatively low. Still, the garrison repulsed an assault on August 22, but the French boats were largely destroyed. There seemed no point in further resistance, and, on the night of August 27, Bougainville and his men slipped away to Montréal. The Richelieu River front had collapsed.

The western St Lawrence River

Montréal was connected to Lake Ontario by the western part of the St Lawrence River. This was a vital waterway as it led to the forts on lakes Ontario and Erie, and from the early 1750s, to the new forts built on the way to the Ohio Valley. From the early 1700s until the last years of the French regime, this route was secure, although there were a few forts along its shores. Heading west, there was a small fort at Les Cèdres on the St Lawrence, about 30 km (18.6 mi) west of the island of Montréal. It was described by John Defever in 1752 as a "small pickett fort where there was only one officer and six men" and where the last French settlements on the river ended. The next post, in the area of the present

Fort La Présentation, c. 1757. This heavily idealized plate after a drawing by the Seigneur de Courville shows the fort and its surroundings. The structures depicted are evocations of the main features and are not meant to show details with accuracy. The fort is shown with its four towers and connecting stockades with the ditch dug in 1756 visible just outside. To the right of the fort is a swamp, and to its left are the longhouses of the Indian village enclosed by a stockade. On the Oswegatchie River is the sawmill near some rapids. The old and usually abandoned trading post of La Galette is shown across the St Lawrence River (bottom right). Sometimes known by its Indian name of Oswegatchie, Fort La Présentation was also often known as "La Galette" because of the latter's proximity. Fort La Présentation was abandoned and dismantled in August 1759. On July 14, 1760, a party of French troops set fire to its remains, but it does not seem to have been entirely destroyed as British troops later occupied the place. Private collection.

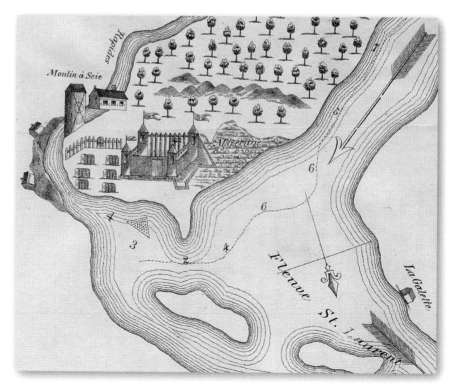

40

town of Prescott, Ontario, was a small trading fort called "La Galette," said to have been built as early as 1682, then abandoned and reoccupied several times.

Fort La Présentation (now Ogdensburg, NY) was begun on June 2, 1749. Its site, which appears to have had a small mission as early as 1718, had a good harbor. It was located at the meeting of the St Lawrence River and the Oswegatchie River, whose source lay in the Iroquois Indians domain to the south. It was often called "La Galette" because of the proximity of the old trade fort on the north shore of the St Lawrence. The strategic location could prevent Anglo-Americans from coming up by the Oswegatchie River and check their movements from Fort Oswego farther west on Lake Ontario. Most of all, Fort La Présentation was designed to reconcile the Iroquois to the French and Christianize them. Its leading figure was the missionary priest François Piquet who actively encouraged war parties to strike the English settlements.

The first fort initially consisted of a small house and a barn, and it had only three soldiers for a garrison. A wooden stockade was built after it was raided in fall 1749 by Indians, who set fire to its barn; they were initially said to be Mohawks, but Governor General de La Jonquière later reported they were in fact Abenaquis who were trying to steal supplies. The fort was expanded in 1750 on a larger plan that contained quarters for the commandant, the missionary, the storekeeper, and for a larger detachment of Compagnie franches de la Marine. The new fort consisted of four large timber towers built on masonry foundations connected by wooden palisades. It was a remarkably

The fortified shipyard at Pointe-au-Baril, 1759–1760 (top) and its location on the St Lawrence on a map (bottom) oriented from east to west. The mission fort of La Présentation (now Ogdensburg, NY) is to the left on the southern shore of the St Lawrence River. After an old print in the *1937 Guide to Fort Wellington*.

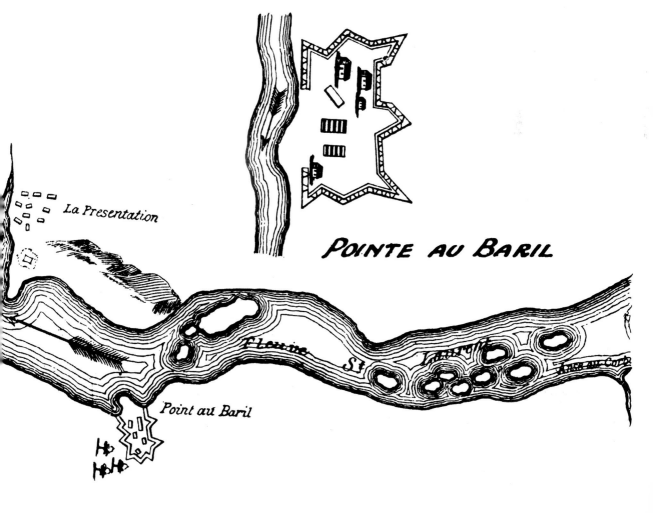

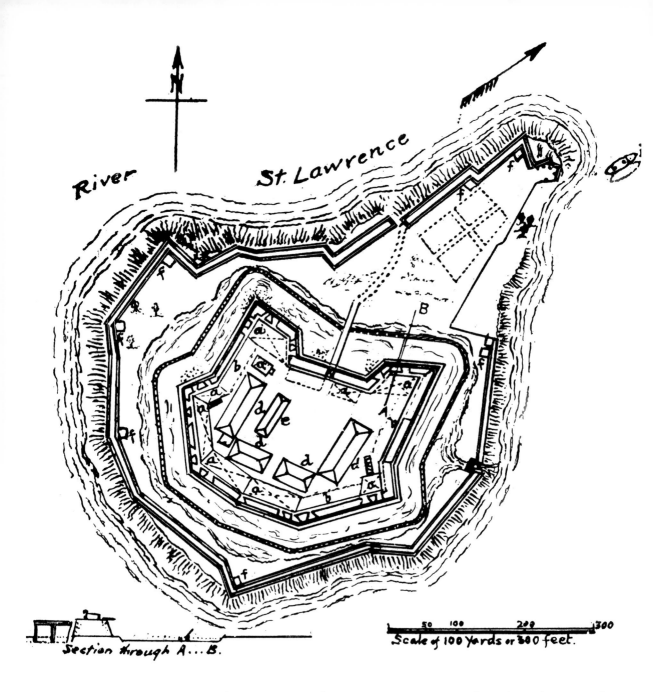

Fort Lévis, 1759–1760. The key to the letters is: a: casemates covered on top but open at sides; b: casemates not covered; c: powder magazine; d: barracks; e: armorer's and smith's shops; f: guns without trunions sunk in solid pieces of timber; g: redoubt, one-log thick; h: harbor for vessels; i: the two vessels; j: the breach. Sections A to B show the elevation in the bottom left. Plan based on Pouchot's plan in the *1937 Guide to Fort Wellington.*

attractive arrangement that was meant to impress the Indians, but certainly could not withstand anything like a siege by an Anglo-American army equipped with artillery. A sawmill was built nearby. Friendly Iroquois were encouraged to settle near the fort, and this idea was a great success. From six families in 1749, the Indian community had grown to 396 families in 1751, and they had to be distributed among three villages. Three years later, the villages had some 49 bark cabins, each from 60 to 80 ft long and with lodging for three to four families, of which about 20 cabins were next to the fort. In 1756, Joseph Eastburn, who had been captured by Indians and taken to La Présentation, mentioned that a trench was being built around the village.

Following the capture and dismantling of Fort Frontenac and its shipyard in August 1758, a small shipyard was established at Pointe-au-Baril on the

north shore of the St Lawrence at about 9 km (5.5 mi) west of La Présentation (near Brockville, ON). The barques *Iroquoise* and *Outaouaise* were launched there the following year. The place was fortified, being protected by earthworks with an outer palisade 10–12 ft high. During 1759, it became obvious to the French that a very strong Anglo-American army would eventually come to the area in 1759 from Lake Ontario. In August, any useful items in Fort La Présentation were moved to an island to block the St Lawrence River. The fort and its mission were dismantled and abandoned.

The small, low-lying, rocky Isle Royale, also known as Orakointon (now named Chimney Island), situated in midstream of the St Lawrence about 6 km (3.7 mi) east of La Présentation, was chosen as the place on which to build Fort Lévis from September 1759. The fort consisted of a large, earthen and wood redoubt with the head of a hornwork facing west, the demi-bastions facing east. The fort was armed with 12 12-pdrs, two 8-pdrs, 13 4-pdrs, four 1-pdrs, all of iron, and four brass 6-pdrs. There were also a few old iron cannons with trunions broken off set in logs. In August 1760, it had a garrison of about 340 French regulars and Canadian militiamen under Captain Pierre Pouchot to face the 11,000 men of General Amherst's army moving east on the St Lawrence. On August 17, the *Outaouaise* was taken by five British rowed galleys after a gallant fight near La Présentation and Pointe-au-Baril, previously abandoned by the French, and it was occupied by Anglo-American troops the same day. General Amherst had a number of siege batteries set up on shore and adjacent islands. After a week of bombardment during which the French managed to wreck a large British vessel, the garrison surrendered on August 25 when the British breached the walls.

Fort Presqu'Île, c. 1754. This bastioned fort was built of squared timber rather than of the usual structures of standing logs and earth that were often put up by the French and English. From a 1930s painting by J. M. Plavcan. Erie Maritime Museum, Erie, Pennsylvania.

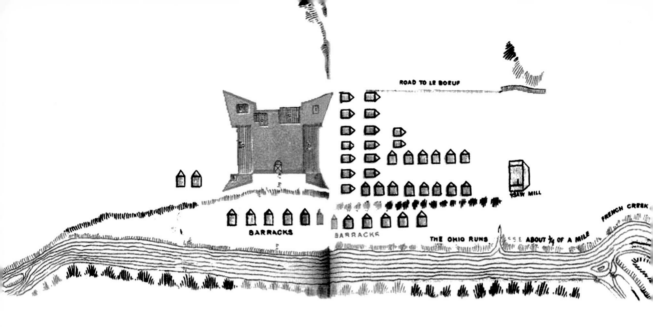

A crude but fairly accurate plan of Fort Machault, c. 1754–1759. This fort was also known as Venango. The two western bastions are correctly shown as larger than those facing the Allegheny River. The comments with this plan, which appear to have been made by an Anglo-American observer, described the fort as being "situated on a rising piece of ground, on a rich bottom, abounding with clover, sixty yards west of the Ohio [actually its confluent, the Allegheny]. The north and south polygon is forty-five yards, and the east and west polygon thirty-seven yards. The bastions are built of saplings, eight inches thick, and thirteen feet in length, set stockade fashion.
Part of the curtains is hewed timber, laid lengthwise upon one another, which also make one side of the barracks." Outside the fort were more barracks along the river and a large Indian village. Plate reproduced in *The Frontier Forts of Western Pennsylvania*, 1916.

The Ohio Valley
From Lake Erie to the Forks

The French claimed that the famous explorer Robert Cavelier de La Salle explored the Ohio River in the late 17th century, something that has yet to be substantiated, as no account of such a journey is known. However, the French eventually learned that this route took one from Lake Erie to the Ohio River, which flowed into the Mississippi. The British naturally rejected the French claims to the Ohio Valley and considered the area within their own sphere of influence. Until the mid-18th century, neither the French nor the Anglo-Americans were often seen in the valley. Communications between Canada and Louisiana usually went west to lakes Erie and Michigan and down the Mississippi by smaller connecting rivers. As communications between Canada and upper Louisiana (or Illinois) increased in importance, the vital position of the Ohio River became apparent to the French.

Increasingly frequent reports of Anglo-American traders roaming into the Ohio Valley reached Governor General de La Galissonière, who became alarmed at this news. His strategic eye perceived the negative effects that would result from cutting the Ohio communications link through gradual penetration of Anglo-Americans into the interior. When the War of Austrian Succession ended in 1748, attention turned to the Ohio. An expedition of some 30 soldiers and 180 militiamen with a few Indians left Montréal for the Ohio led by Captain Céléron de Blainville in June 1749. They roamed about the Allegheny and Ohio valleys burying lead plates along its shores to indicate the territory was France's. However, the Anglo-Americans were not impressed by lead plates. Nothing further was done for the next few years as Anglo-American traders penetrated deeper into traditional zones of French influence. But in 1753, large parties of French soldiers and Canadian militiamen arrived on the southern shore of Lake Erie and went down the rivers to the Ohio, building forts along the way.

Fort Presqu'Ile was built on the southern shore of Lake Erie from May 15, 1753 (now Erie, PA). It was, according to Father François Forget Duberger, a missionary who saw it in July 1754, 180 ft square, while gunner Joseph Charles Bonin mentions its four bastions had 12 guns. The walls were built of squared chestnut logs. A novel aspect to this fort was that the timber logs

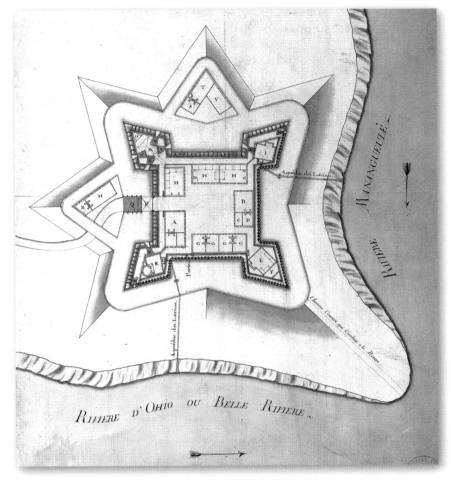

A French plan of Fort Duquesne, 1754. This plan, probably made by colonial artillery Captain François Le Mercier, is the only definitive one and the only reliable source of information about the use of the buildings in the fort. It shows the fort oriented to the east (top). The artillery is concentrated in the northeast bastion with four guns and the possibility of a fifth mounted en barbette at its point. A land attack was obviously mostly to be expected in that area, the northwest and the southeast bastions having two guns each. The southwest bastion looking toward the meeting of the rivers had no guns. The letters indicate the following areas: A: commandant's quarters, B: storekeeper's room, C: small store, D: distribution, E: cadets' quarters, F: jail, G: officers' and chaplain's rooms, H: barracks, I: blacksmith's shop, K: bakery, L: latrines, M: powder magazine, N: platforms, O: barbette platform, P: drawbridge, Q: fixed outer bridge, R: interpreter's quarters, S: surgeon's quarters, T: hospital, V: storehouse. Bibliothèque Nationale, Paris, Ge D 8049.

were laid flat one on top of the other rather than the usual vertical stockade made with logs planted into the ground. Four buildings were inside, and a masonry powder magazine was added later. This fort's main purpose was to act as a supply depot between forts to the east and the new forts being built farther south. Its usual garrison was about 150 men.

Fort Le Boeuf (now Waterford, PA) was built from July 11, 1753, near the shores of the small *"rivière aux Boeufs"* ("French Creek" to the Anglo-Americans) at the end of a 9-mile portage from Fort Presqu'Ile. It was a smaller fort, 90 ft square according to Father Duberger, built of beech with the back of its buildings acting as walls and the bastions made of logs planted into the ground. It already had eight guns mounted by December. It was intended as a link and supply depot on the route to the Ohio.

Fort Machault, also known as Fort Venango, was started in August 1753. Its name came from the then-current minister of the French Navy, the Count de Machault. The fort was situated on the Allegheny River, just south of its confluence with French Creek (now Franklin, PA). This was a good location and had been previously used, possibly as early as 1741, by John Fraser, a trader and blacksmith. With the French coming down, Fraser prudently left the place in May 1753. The French took over his cabins, sheds, and blacksmith shop in August and started putting up their fort. It was an important depot site, larger than Fort Le Boeuf, having a rectangular layout with large bastions, the two western ones having perimeters of 135 ft and the eastern ones 111 ft

FORT LE BOEUF, 1753–1758

Built by the French in summer 1753, Fort Le Boeuf was reached by young George Washington to deliver the summons of Virginia's Governor Dinwiddie. Washington described the fort as having "four houses [which] compose the sides; the Bastions are made of Piles driven into the Ground, and about 12 feet above, and sharp at Top, with Port Holes cut for Cannon and Loop Holes for the small Arms to fire through. There are eight 6 lb. pieces mounted, two in each Bastion, and one Piece of four Pound before the Gate; in the Bastions are a Guard House, Chapel, Doctor's Lodging, and the Commander's private store, round which are laid Eight Forms for the Cannon and Men to stand on; There are several barracks without the Fort, for the Soldiers Dwelling, covered, some with Bark, and some with Boards, and made chiefly, such as Stables, Etc."

(English measures). There were six swivel guns in the bastions. Long, square-log buildings formed the northern and southern walls while stockades formed the east and west walls and the bastions. Next to the fort was a sizable Indian village named Venango, a corruption of the Seneca name *In-Nan-Ga-eh*.

In Virginia, Governor Robert Dinwiddie considered that the French were seizing British territory. If nothing was done about it, French forts would legitimize by mere occupation their claims, and the area would be lost to Britain, especially to Virginia. Dinwiddie sent young Major George Washington to deliver a summons. He made the long journey into the wilderness to Fort Le Boeuf, and in December 1753, Washington delivered Governor Dinwiddie's letters to Commandant Le Gardeur de Saint-Pierre, "a Knight of the Military Order of St Louis" whom he described as an "elderly Gentleman, and has much the Air of a Soldier."

For both sides, the summons was the signal to occupy the area as fast as possible. In spring 1754, Washington, newly promoted to lieutenant colonel, commanded 132 Virginia provincial soldiers heading toward the confluence of the Allegheny, Monongahela, and Ohio rivers. He stayed at Great Meadows with most of his men, but a detachment went on to what would become the city of Pittsburgh and started building a fort. Several days later, on April 16, a force of some 600 French soldiers and Canadian militiamen under the command of Claude Pécaudy de Contrecoeur arrived at that strategic spot and ordered the Virginians to withdraw immediately, which they did. Contrecoeur's men then continued to build the fort, adapting it to their own design, which they named Fort Duquesne. The new French fort was built on a square plan with four bastions and a dry ditch. It was small, incapable of sustaining an attack by an enemy equipped with siege artillery, expensive to maintain, and at the far end of a very long supply line. However, it achieved its primary purpose: to secure the Ohio for France. In a frontier context, this fort, together with its relaying

The outline of the 1754–1758 Fort Duquesne is marked on the ground of the memorial park at the confluence of the Monongahela and Ohio Rivers in Pittsburgh. The eastern face measures about 154 ft (English measure) between the tips of the bastions and about 160 ft (English measure) in the other direction. A dry ditch, now filled and covered by grass, surrounded the fort.

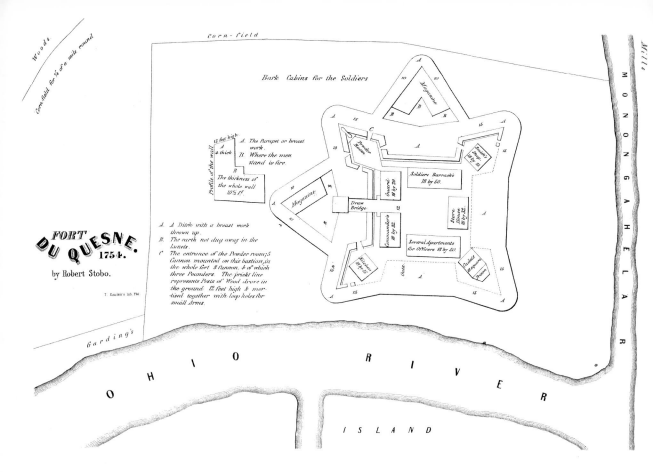

Plan of Fort Duquesne in 1754
after a sketch by Robert Stobo,
a Virginia officer detained
there. This remarkably detailed
plan shows, with a dotted line,
the fort's ramparts still under
construction on the sides of the
Ohio and Monongahela rivers.
The finished earthen wall was
about 12 ft high with the
parapet 4 ft wide at the top
and 10½ ft at the bottom.
Print after Robert Stobo.
Private collection.

forts along the way from Lake Erie, was far stronger than anything the colonial Americans could bring against it.

The stage was set for confrontation, and that is exactly what occurred in the Ohio. The ambush and killing of French Ensign Jummonville and his truce party by Washington's Virginians in May 1754 was followed by the capture of the Virginians' Fort Necessity by Jummonville's brother, Captain Coulon de Villiers the following month. This was tantamount to war, and both France and Britain sent regular battalions to their respective colonies. The British force under General Edward Braddock was to take Fort Duquesne, but it was wiped out at the Monongahela River on July 9, 1755, a few miles east of Fort Duquesne, by a mixed force of Indians, French colonial troops, and Canadian militiamen. Thereafter, the fort served as a base for raiding parties, especially by allied Indians. An Anglo-American attempt to win the Ohio Valley was made again in 1758 with a mixed British and American army of about 7,000 men under the command of Major General John Forbes marching on Fort Duquesne. The lessons of Monongahela were such that, in spite of having three times as many men as General Braddock had, General Forbes was extremely patient and methodical, systematically building a road with relaying forts over the wilderness. He nevertheless had difficulties, notably when his vanguard of 800 men under Major James Grant was crushed by French troops from Fort Duquesne in September and by French raids on Fort Ligonier the following months. Ultimately, Forbes' road got within a few miles of Fort Duquesne, which its French garrison blew up as they retreated to Lake Erie on November 26, 1758.

The Ottawa River Valley and Hudson's Bay

The Ottawa River flows from the northwest to meet the St Lawrence at Montréal. Until the mid-19th century, the Ottawa River was the main "highway" of the Canadian fur trade. Thanks to a network of lakes and rivers coming from the west that connected with the Ottawa River at the Mattawa fork, it formed a route that reached the northern shore of Lake Huron. This gave access to the *Pays d'en Haut* – the Upper Country – by lakes Michigan and Superior and all their tributary rivers that could take one as far as the Great Plains or the Gulf of Mexico. Furthermore, by continuing north on the Mattawa fork on the Ottawa River, one would reach the fur-rich Témiscamingue and Abitibi areas, and beyond that Hudson's Bay. Thus, the Ottawa River was a very busy highway; groups of canoes called "brigades" were constantly moving back and forth loaded with furs going east and all sorts of European goods going west. There was also a great deal of vital military activity on this route, as it was also the highway for garrisons and military supplies to reach the many frontier forts farther away.

Although very valuable, this waterway had very few military fortifications on its route, and nearly all of them were near Montréal. Even during the 17th-century wars, the route was considered relatively secure because the hostile Iroquois Indians were farther south and the English much farther north at Hudson's Bay. The Ottawa River and its tributaries mostly had a number of trade forts, usually made up of log cabins surrounded by a stockade that acted more as a fence against animals or lone, human predators. When the canoe brigades left Lachine near Montréal and crossed the portage

The evacuation of Fort Duquesne by the French troops, November 24, 1758. Brigadier General John Forbes' numerous Anglo-American armies progressed slowly but surely across western Pennsylvania toward Fort Duquesne during 1758. By late fall, it was clear to French commander De Lignery that his small garrison could not resist the approaching overwhelming enemy force. On the night of November 24, the fort was evacuated, set on fire, and blown up with some 50 barrels of gunpowder. Print after W. P. Snyder.

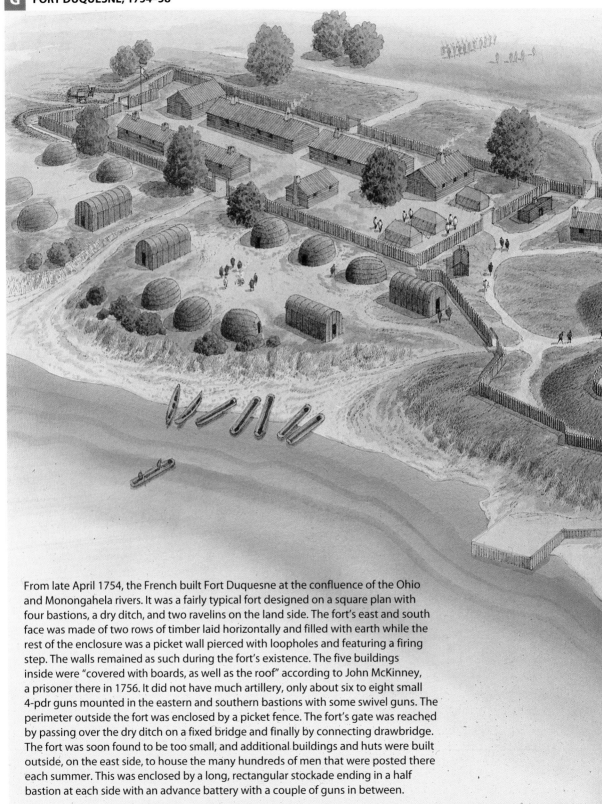

From late April 1754, the French built Fort Duquesne at the confluence of the Ohio and Monongahela rivers. It was a fairly typical fort designed on a square plan with four bastions, a dry ditch, and two ravelins on the land side. The fort's east and south face was made of two rows of timber laid horizontally and filled with earth while the rest of the enclosure was a picket wall pierced with loopholes and featuring a firing step. The walls remained as such during the fort's existence. The five buildings inside were "covered with boards, as well as the roof" according to John McKinney, a prisoner there in 1756. It did not have much artillery, only about six to eight small 4-pdr guns mounted in the eastern and southern bastions with some swivel guns. The perimeter outside the fort was enclosed by a picket fence. The fort's gate was reached by passing over the dry ditch on a fixed bridge and finally by connecting drawbridge. The fort was soon found to be too small, and additional buildings and huts were built outside, on the east side, to house the many hundreds of men that were posted there each summer. This was enclosed by a long, rectangular stockade ending in a half bastion at each side with an advance battery with a couple of guns in between.

The capture of Fort Nelson (York Factory) by Pierre Le Moyne d'Iberville and his men in 1697. This is the fort rebuilt in 1691 with four tower-like bastions holding the artillery. It was no match for an enemy that had mortars, as seen by the two flaming bombs coming down on the fort. Renamed Fort Bourbon following its surrender, it remained under the French flag until 1713. Print after Bacqueville de La Potherie. Library and Archives Canada, C113194.

near Fort Senneville, they then went across the Lac des Deux-Montagnes – the Lake of Two Mountains – and came upon the Fort des Deux-Montagnes, a fortified Indian mission established in 1721 (now Oka, Québec) that had a small regular garrison. At the time of its foundation, the missionary Sulpician Order had agreed to build a stone fort within seven years, but the fortification plan drawn up by Chief Engineer Chaussegros de Léry was denounced by the fathers as being far too expensive to realize. A small wooden fort with an adjoining stockade enclosed the Indian village until the 1740s, when a stone fort surrounded by a ditch was built by the Sulpicians. It was described in 1752 by Engineer Franquet as having walls 12 ft high pierced with loopholes and featuring three bastions covering the landward sides, and a stockade facing the lake. Within were a church and the priest's residence. Franquet considered the fort incapable of stopping a strong enemy force. The adjoining Indian village had over 200 warriors, half being Algonquins and Nipissings and half being allied Iroquois. On the whole, allied Indians probably provided the best defense potential on the Ottawa.

Then came Fort du Long-Sault, a small trade post in the 18th century that had been the scene of a desperate battle to save Montréal in 1660. Dollard des Ormeaux, the commander of the small Montréal garrison, left the town in May with 17 French companions to patrol the Ottawa River and ambush small Iroquois parties. At Long-Sault, they found an abandoned stockade Indian fort that they tried to repair with the help of 40 Huron and four Algonquin allied Indians who joined them. Soon thereafter, some 200 enemy Onondaga Iroquois came down the river and attacked the fort several times but were repulsed with heavy losses. Some 500 Mohawk arrived reinforcements, according to French accounts, while most Hurons defected to the Iroquois. In spite of that, new assaults also failed but the humiliated Iroquois persisted. The end came when Dollard threw a powder keg (or a musket filled with powder) on the assaulting masses, but it hit a branch and fell back into the fort. The garrison was massacred. However, it was said that the losses inflicted by Dollard and his companions on the Iroquois were such that it discouraged them from attacking

Montréal. This account has been the subject of much debate, but it does seem that Dollard and his men, through a conjunction of circumstances, did divert a large Iroquois force from attacking the Montréal area. The exact location of the fort where this heroic fight took place remains speculative.

At the end of the 17th century, another Fort du Long-Sault with an occasional small garrison was built to control illegal trading, with a companion post on the opposite shore of the Ottawa River. Both later became trading posts. Farther up the river were the trade forts of Carillon, La Petite-Nation, and Du Lièvre, the great portage at the Chaudière Falls (now the cities of Ottawa and Gatineau) where one would find log huts near the shore but no fortifications. Fort Du Moine came next, a fortified trading post above Ile-aux-Allumettes. Farther up was Fort Coulonge, a stockade work apparently built in the 1680s and certainly before 1695. This was the main trade fort in the area, and it also occasionally housed troops in transit to forts on the shores of the Great Lakes.

The river went on north of the Matawa fork, and at the broadening of its course to the width of a lake was Fort Témiscamingue in the upper Ottawa Valley, a structure that may date from as early as 1677. This was the main fort for the French fur trade between the upper Ottawa and Hudson's Bay and was mentioned as a "house" on a small island with 14 traders when soldiers and militiamen of the Chevalier de Troye's expedition to Hudson's Bay passed by there in 1686. It appears to have been abandoned due to hostile Indians two years later. In 1720, it was back in operation and may have had as many as 60 men in the 1750s although very few would have been troops. The hardy traders and voyagers at these posts were also, by law, militiamen. Fort Abitibi was built in three days on a hill near Lake Abitibi by De Troye's expedition in June 1686 and described as a stockade log work with four small bastions. It was a post dependent on Fort Témiscamingue, 120 leagues (roughly 420 mi) away. In 1758, the 100 men making up the "garrisons" of both forts were withdrawn, although a few traders remained.

Hudson's Bay

The English explorer Henry Hudson had a house built at the mouth of the Rupert River in 1610, and although the bay would bear his name, the area was claimed by both Britain and France until 1713. In 1668, Fort Charles (renamed Fort Rupert in 1670) was built for English traders on the site of Hudson's house; its buildings were of stone protected by a stockade. Two years later, the area was

Priests from several Catholic Church orders were active in New France from the early 17th century, many of them residing in forts. They had the dual role of being a chaplain to the fort's inhabitants as well as being a missionary to the Indians. During the reign of Louis XIV, a branch of the Franciscan Order, the Récollets, became predominant as Navy chaplains. In 1670, Récollets fathers arrived in Canada. Their numbers grew rapidly, with many Canadians entering the order. In 1692, they were officially appointed by the king to be chaplains of the troops in Canada and Newfoundland, a duty that many had been fullfilling for some time. In practice, Récollets fathers were usually found in the larger forts of the northeast. Being a "poor" order, their cross was made of plain wood suspended by a rosary of small wooden balls. They wore a dark gray or black rough cloth habit with a white cord at the waist and wooden sandals in the summer, as shown in this period print. They had appropriate footwear and cloaks in the winter. Private collection.

53

A map of the forts of Hudson's Bay and Upper Ottawa. The names of the forts of Hudson's Bay refer to the period during which they were occupied by the French (1686–1713).

The forts of Hudson's Bay and Upper Ottawa

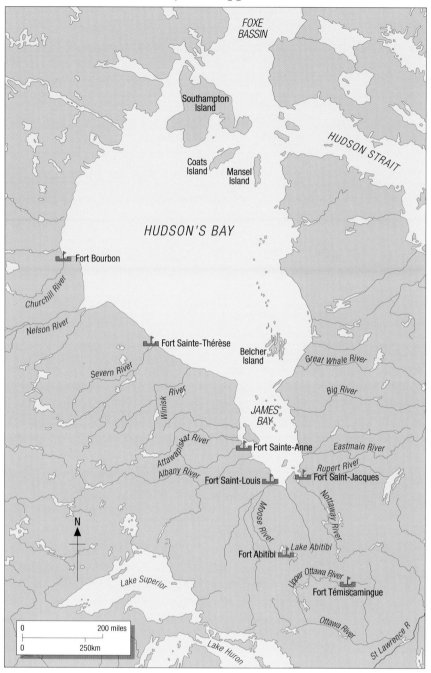

granted by King Charles II to the Hudson's Bay Company (HBC), and Fort Nelson (or Fort York) was built at the mouth of the Nelson River, abandoned and rebuilt in 1682 at Woodchuck Creek, and destroyed by French traders in 1683. Since 1682, the French had built Fort Bourbon on the Nelson River, and it was seized by the English in 1683. The HBC had four forts on the bay a year later.

The French retorted in 1686 with a major expedition under the command of the Chevalier de Troyes and Pierre Le Moyne d'Iberville. From then until the 1713 Treaty of Utrecht that granted Hudson's Bay to Britain, the forts were taken, retaken and changed names many times as follows:

Fort Charles (Fort Rupert or Rupert House from 1670): held by English: 1668–1686 and 1693–1697; held by French as Fort Saint-Jacques: 1686–1693 and 1697–1713.

Fort Nelson (later York Factory): "a very solid fort with six cannons" according to Pierre Radisson in 1682, rebuilt with four bastions from 1691; held by English: 1670–1694 and 1696–1697; held by French as Fort Bourbon: 1694–1696 and 1697–1713.

Fort Moose: square stockade 100 ft to each side with four bastions; held by English: 1671–1686 and 1693–1694; held by French as Fort Saint-Louis, Fort Monsipi, and Fort Monsoni: 1686–1693 and 1694–1713.

Fort Albany: a strong work with four bastions and 43 guns; held by English: 1683–1686, 1689–1692 and 1693–1713; held by French as Fort Sainte-Anne: 1686–1689 and 1692–1693.

Fort Severn: of logs with four bastions held by English: 1685–1689 and 1693–1694; held by French as Fort Sainte-Thérèse or Neuve-Savane: 1689–1693 and 1694–1713.

The end of the Seven Years War in the Northeast

The end of the war came in the St Lawrence Valley. Haviland's force coming up the Richelieu met James Murray's coming from Québec and Jeffery Amherst's arriving on the western St Lawrence, all three armies uniting outside the walls of Montréal in early September. For General Lévis, his officers, and his men within the city, there was no point in further bloodshed. On September 8, the remnants of the valiant French forces surrendered after burning the regimental colors. In a most ungracious display, General Amherst had refused granting the Honors of War to the hard-fighting French troops, and an offended General Lévis thus put a check to Amherst's cupidity. In the following days and weeks, outlying garrisons were relieved by British troops.

One small group isolated on the borderlands of Acadia did not surrender immediately. In February 1761, General Murray wrote to General Amherst

Very little is known of the fort at Long-Sault where Dollard des Ormeaux and his companions perished after a desperate fight in May 1660. It was described as an existing "small Indian fort" that was made of "bad, worthless logs" and "commanded by a nearby height." It is also known to have had musket loopholes. Dollard's party occupied it, having nothing better in which to seek shelter. In their final assault, the Iroquois used "mantlets of three pieces of wood lashed side by side, which covered them from the crown of the head to the middle of the thigh" according to chronicler Dollier de Casson. A gory sight was the heads of Iroquois Indians, killed in previous assaults, which were put on stakes. Mural painting of the final assault done in the 1930s by Topham at the City of Montréal's Mount Royal chalet.

The plain white naval ensign was ordered to be hoisted on French warships and forts from 1661, as seen at Fort Chambly. It was also extensively used in the inland forts of New France. Today considered the "surrender flag," it was very much a fighting flag in pre-1790 France. This stemmed from the practice of hoisting the enemy's color when suing for a capitulation, which, for Britons and Anglo-Americans, meant putting up the French white flag. The practice became generalized after France's tricolor flag replaced this white ensign in the early 1790s. On the right, note the wooden guérite occasionally used in Canadian forts.

that Lieutenant de Niverville, commanding a dozen soldiers of the colonial troops "still in arms… at a post some distance from Ristigouche," would not surrender and even "disclaimed the capitulation as it had not been formally communicated to him." It finally was communicated officially, and this small post in the Miramichi area may have been the last in the northeast to be abandoned by its undaunted little French garrison.

THE FORT GARRISONS

The early garrisons of New France were made up of soldiers enlisted in the service of the monopoly companies, such as the Company of the Hundred Associates, to whom the territory was granted by the royal crown for exploitation and colonization. As soldiers were expensive, they were few in number until 1665 when King Louis XIV sent 1,200 regulars from the Royal Army. These troops built and garrisoned the Richelieu Valley forts, but, by 1671, New France had only a few dozen soldiers again. In 1683, renewed warfare in Canada brought the first three of many infantry companies to

Barrack room interior, c. 1690s–1750s. By regulation, a barrack room for French troops was to have a table with two benches and as many beds as could be fitted in. This reconstruction at Fort Carillon (now Ticonderoga) shows a table and its benches made according to designs shown in the manuscript *Livre des Fortifications* compiled by the Seigneur de Masse from 1687 to 1728, with measurements according to Mr de Chenevière's 1742 *Détails Militaires*. The double bunk beds are not regulation but follow those made at Louisbourg and most likely at other forts, such as Carillon or Duquesne, where lodging space was at a premium.

New France, this time as permanent garrisons. They eventually were known as Compagnies franches de la Marine – independent companies of the Navy. They were on the establishment of the French Navy's colonial troops. This was because, since the later 1660s, the administration of colonies in America was the responsibility of the Ministry of the Navy.

By 1688, the number of companies had risen to 35 but was subsequently reduced to 28 and remained at that number until 1750 when two more companies were added. Company strength was initially at 50 men each, but this varied over the years. Acadia's first company of troops arrived in 1685, a second in 1696, and there were four from 1702 to 1710. Placentia had its first company in 1687, its second in 1694, and a third from 1696 to 1713. From 1713, Isle Royale had seven companies, then six from 1722 when

Fort Chambly National Historic Site during a lovely fall day. The old stone fort of 1710 has been totally restored by Parks Canada and is now invaded by hordes of visitors enjoying this unique heritage structure and the park that surrounds it.

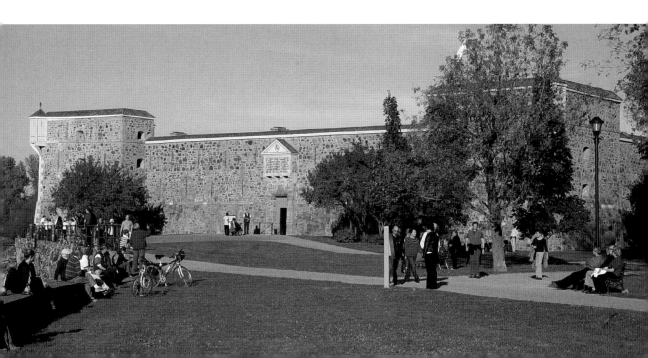

BELOW

Soldier of the Compagnies franches de la Marine in New France, 1680s. From 1683, soldiers from these independent companies garrisoned New France's cities and forts. Soldiers were issued this grey-white uniform with blue cuffs and brass buttons and were all armed, from about 1685, with flintlock muskets (except for the garrison of Placentia, Newfoundland, which had matchlocks). After 1700, the uniforms of the troops in Acadia and Placentia were different from those issued in Canada. Reconstitution by Michel Pétard. Parks Canada.

Fort Light Artillery

A breech-loading wrought iron swivel gun found at Fort Saint-Frédéric. These medieval-looking small cannons remained popular as antipersonnel weapons in the Navy well into the 18th century and could be found in almost every fort in New France. They were relatively light, easy to transport, could be made in Canada by a well-equipped master blacksmith, and indeed, some were made in Montréal. Crown Point State Historic Site, Crown Point, NY.

a detachment of the Karrer Swiss Regiment was added in Louisbourg. The number of Compagnies franches was raised to eight in 1730 and 24 in 1750, but nearly all were posted to Fortress Louisbourg with only a few squads detached at Port Toulouse, Port Dauphin, and Isle Saint-Jean. This was not the case with other garrisons, notably the companies in Canada, whose officers and men were detached far and wide in small groups.

In the late 17th century, both officers and men came from France, but fairly rapidly, Canadian-born officers were appointed and formed about half of the officer corps in Canada by the 1720s and the great majority by the middle of the 18th century. Many were renowned for their ability in bush warfare. The enlisted men continued to be recruited in France and sent to New France, in the hope that many would settle after their service.

A soldier in the Compagnies franches enlisted for a period of 6 years, although this might be extended because of the lack of replacement recruits arriving from France. Those posted in forts along the St Lawrence and Richelieu Rivers and Lake Champlain appear to have been in fairly comfortable circumstances. The Swedish scientist Pehr Kalm gave a glowing account of the life of the troops he saw at Fort Saint-Frédéric in 1749, who had "such advantages here, [as] they are not allowed in every part of the world." Besides generous rations, the lake close by offered excellent fishing and "the woods abound with birds and animals" so that those who "chose to be diligent, may live extremely well, and very grand in regards to food." They were also paid for extra labor so that, concluded Kalm, "it is not surprising to find the men are very fresh, well fed, strong and lively here." When they were discharged from the service, the soldiers were given assistance to settle and build their homes. Many did so in the seigneuries held by their former officers, some within view of a fort such as Chambly or Sorel, which they had garrisoned. In many cases, their wives were the nearby settler's daughter they had courted when serving at the fort. There are no precise statistics on the settlement of soldiers of the Compagnies franches, but a reasonable

figure would be at least 3,000 from 1683 to 1760. Compagnies franches soldiers were not the only ones to garrison forts. They were often joined by reinforcements of Canadian militiamen, usually in wartime and mostly during the summer.

Initially, soldiers posted in forts often had to lodge in "huts made of stakes covered with bark or with boards" with most "sleeping on straw" according to a 1695 report. In the 18th century, conditions improved, at least in large forts such as Chambly or Carillon. In those forts, it seems that an effort was made to meet the royal regulations on lodging soldiers, which required a table and two benches and as many beds as each barrack room could hold. Barrack beds were supposed to have space for three infantry soldiers (actually two because the third was on guard, according to the official logic). Regulation beds were to be made of oak or other hardwood and measured 1.3 m (4.3 English feet) wide, 1.8 m (5.9 English feet) long, and stood 32–40 cm (12.6–15.7 English inches) high. They were garnished by a linen mattress filled with wool, a palliasse (a hard straw mattress), a bolster stuffed with wool or straw, two linen sheets, and a white woolen blanket with a fleur-de-lis embroidered at its center. In New France, it appears that narrower double-tier bunk beds were used as well. In Louisbourg, such beds capable of accommodating two soldiers per level were used. It seems most likely that double-tier beds were put in other forts, such as Carillon, where space was at a premium. In most of the larger forts, the number of men in garrison was relatively low in the winter but increased during the summer.

Daily life in these forts was the usual routine of parades, guard-mounts, and fatigues as in any garrison in Europe. In North America however, what lay outside the fort's perimeter was a totally alien environment. In most cases, the fort was isolated and surrounded by a vast primeval forest where an enemy Indian might be lurking, unseen. This was especially the case in 17th-century Canada. By the 18th century, the tables had turned in favor of the French and Canadians who now mastered the intricacies of wilderness warfare. Patrols in the fort's area by soldiers, Canadian militiamen, and allied Indians were added to the garrison's routine. Desertion was relatively rare and unattractive to soldiers in Canada, no doubt due to the prospect of having to travel great distances through wilderness to reach the relatively alien English colonies while being pursued by allied Indians and Canadian militiamen.

The imposing restored stone walls of Fort Carillon, renamed Fort Ticonderoga in 1759, as seen from the east. Situated on a height surrounded by mountains and lakes, Fort Ticonderoga is one of the most scenic and spectacular historic sites in the United States today.

THE FORTS TODAY

Nearly all the forts cited in this study are now commemorated by the various federal, provincial, and state governments in Canada and the United States. These range from simple site markers to full restorations or reconstructions. In Canada, the forts that have undergone the most restorations are in Parks Canada's National Historic Sites network, and these often have good visitor services and interpretations. In the United States, the French forts are usually administered by state historic site agencies and nonprofit associations, and their efforts are especially notable in New York and Pennsylvania. Most forts can easily be reached by car, thanks to the network of interstate highways in the Northeast. A drive north from Castine (Maine) along the coast goes through St John (New Brunswick), reaches Fort Beauséjour, and by turning east, goes into Nova Scotia's Annapolis Valley to the reconstructed Port Royal habitation and Fort Anne (French Port Royal before 1710).

Driving south from Montréal, one comes to Fort Chambly on the Richelieu River, an important site both for its beauty and significance in fort architecture. This fort also has a large museum-style interpretation center. Nothing remains of the French forts at Sorel, Saint-Jean, or Isle-aux-Noix although the last two have substantial later forts certainly worth a visit. Heading south of Lake Champlain, one reaches Crown Point State Historic Site with the ruins of Fort Saint-Frédéric and the later British fort with a fine interpretation center. A few miles farther south brings one to Fort Ticonderoga, built by the French as Fort Carillon and one of the major sites in the Northeast due to the extensive restoration that has been underway since the early 1900s. It features a major museum and a fine collection of ordnance situated in a place of outstanding beauty.

The French forts in the upper Ohio are not reconstructed, although, apart from site markers, forts Presqu'Ile and Le Boeuf are interpreted in museum displays. The outline of Fort Duquesne has been traced in a lovely park in Pittsburgh, and its story is told in excellent displays in the State of Pennsylvania's nearby Fort Pitt Museum. All in all, anyone willing to take to the road is not likely to be disappointed by the generally numerous, well-managed sites in the Northeast.

GLOSSARY OF FORTIFICATION TERMS

Abatis A defensive barricade or row of obstructions made up of closely-spaced felled trees, their tops toward the enemy, their branches trimmed to points and interlaced where possible.

Banquette A continuous step or ledge at the interior base of a parapet on which defenders stood to direct musket fire over the top of the wall. A fire step.

Bastion A projection in the enceinte, made up of four sides, two faces and two flanks, which better enabled a garrison to defend the ground adjacent to the main or curtain walls.

Battery An emplacement for artillery.

Berm A line of wooden stakes or logs, 6–8 ft long, planted in the middle of a ditch and pointing vertically.

Breastwork	*See* Parapet.
Casemate	A mortar-bomb or shell-proof chamber located within the walls of defensive works; generally pierced with openings for weapons; loopholes for muskets or embrasures for cannon.
Cordon	The coping or top course of a scarp or a rampart, sometimes of different-colored stone and set proud from the rest of the wall. The point where a rampart stops and a parapet begins.
Counterguard	Defensive work built in a ditch in front of a bastion to give it better protection.
Covered way	A depression, road, or path in the outer edge of a fort's moat or ditch, generally protected from enemy fire by a parapet, at the foot of which might be a banquette enabling the coverage of the glacis with musketry.
Cunette	A furrow located in the bottom of a dry ditch for the purpose of drainage.
Curtain	The wall of a fort between two bastions.
Demi-bastion	A half-bastion with only one face and one flank.
Demi-lune	Triangular-shaped defensive work built in a ditch in front of a bastion or of a curtain wall.
Ditch	A wide, deep trench around a defensive work. When filled with water it was termed a moat or wet ditch; otherwise a dry ditch, or fosse.
Embrasure	An opening in a wall or parapet allowing cannon to fire through it, the gunners remaining under cover. The sides of the embrasure were called "cheeks," the bottom called the "sole," the narrow part of the opening called the "throat," and the wide part called the "splay."
En barbette	An arrangement for cannon to be fired directly over the top of a low wall instead of through embrasures.
Enfilade fire	Fire directed from the flank or side of a body of troops, or along the length of a ditch, parapet, or wall. Guns in the flank of a bastion can direct enfilade fire along the face of the curtain.
Epaulement	A parapet or work protecting against enfilade fire.
Fascines	Long bundles of sticks or small diameter tree branches bound together for use in revetments, for stabilizing earthworks, filling ditches, etc.
Fosse or foss	*See* Ditch.
Fraise	A defense of closely placed stakes or logs, 6–8 ft long, driven or dug into the ground and sharpened; arranged to point horizontally or obliquely outward from a defensive position.
Gabion	A large, round, woven wicker cylinder intended to be set in place and filled with earth, sand, or stones.

Gallery	An interior passageway or corridor that ran along the base of a fort's walls.
Gate	A main entrance to a fortress.
Glacis	A broad, gently sloped earthwork or natural slope in front of a fort, separated from the fort proper by a ditch and outworks and so arranged as to be swept with musket or cannon fire.
Gorge	The interval or space between the two curtain angles of a bastion. In a ravelin, the area formed by the flanked angle and either left open or enclosed.
Guardhouse	The headquarters for the daily guard.
Guérite	A small lookout watchtower, usually located on the upper outer corner of a bastion.
Half bastion	*See* Demi-bastion.
Hornwork	A work made up of a bastion front; two half bastions and a curtain and two long sides termed branches.
Loopholes	Small openings in walls or stockades through which muskets were fired.
Machicoulis	Projections in old castles and over gates, left open above to throw stones, etc. on enemies below. These were built into several forts in Canada.
Magazine	A place for the storage of gunpowder, arms, or goods generally related to ordnance.
Merlon	The solid feature between embrasures in a parapet.
Moat	*See* Ditch.
Orgue	*See* Portcullis.
Outwork	An outer defense, inside the glacis but outside the body of the place. A ravelin is an outwork.
Palisade	A high fence made of stakes, poles, palings, or pickets, supported by rails and set endwise in the ground from 6–9 in. apart. *See* Stockade.
Parapet	A breastwork or protective wall over which defenders, standing on banquettes, fired their weapons.
Portcullis	A timber or iron grating that can be lowered to close the gates of a fortress. Called *"orgue"* (organ) in French.
Postern	A passage leading from the interior of a fortification to the ditch.
Rampart	The mass of earth, usually faced with masonry, formed to protect an enclosed area.
Ravelin	An outwork consisting of two faces forming a salient angle at the front and a flank angle to the rear that was usually closed at the

gorge. Ravelins were separated from the main body of the place by ditches and functioned to protect curtains.

Redoubt	An enclosed fortification without bastions.
Revetment	The sloping wall of stone or brick supporting the outer face of a rampart.
Sallyport	A passageway within the rampart, usually vaulted, leading from the interior of a fort to the exterior, primarily to provide for sorties.
Sap	A trench and parapet constructed by besiegers to protect their approaches toward a fortification.
Scarp	The interior side of a ditch or the outer slope of a rampart.
Stockade	A line or enclosure of logs or stakes set upright in the earth with no separation between them, to form a barrier eight or more feet high. Stockades were generally provided with loopholes. The loopholes were reached by banquettes or elevated walks. *See* Palisade.
Traverse	A parapet or wall thrown across a covered way, a terreplein, ditch, or other location to prevent enfilade or reverse fire along a work.

SELECT BIBLIOGRAPHY

Beaudet, Pierre, and Céline Cloutier, *Archaeology at Fort Chambly*. Ottawa, National Historic Parks and Sites, Canadian Parks Services, 1989.

Castonguay, Jacques, *Les défis du Fort Saint-Jean*. Saint-Jean, Éditions du Richelieu, 1975.

Charbonneau, André, *The Fortifications of Isle-aux-Noix*. Ottawa, Parks Canada, 1994.

Chartrand, René, *Canadian Military Heritage: Volume I: 1000–1754*. Montréal, Art Global, Inc., 1993. (*Canadian Military Heritage* can be downloaded at Canada's Department of National Defense's Canadian Military History Gateway: http://www.cmhg.gc.ca)

Chenevières, François de, *Détails militaires* (two volumes), Paris, Mariette, 1742.

Couillard-Després, A., *Histoire de Sorel*. Montréal, Imprimerie des Sourds Muets, 1926.

Gélinas, Cyrille, *The Role of Fort Chambly in the Development of New France 1665–1760*, Ottawa, National Historic Parks and Sites Branch, Parks Canada, 1983.

Dunn, Guillaume, *Les forts de l'Outaouais*. Montréal, Éditions du Jour, 1975.

Hamilton, Edward P., *Fort Ticonderoga: Key to a Continent*. Boston, Little, Brown, 1964.

Quesada, Alejandro M. de, *A History of Florida Forts*. Charleston, SC, The History Press, 2006.

Roncière, Charles de La, *La Floride française*. Paris, Éditions nationales, 1928.

Roy, Pierre-Georges, *Hommes et choses du Fort Saint-Frédéric*. Montréal, Éditions des Dix, 1946.

Stotz, Charles Morse, *Outpost of the War for Empire*. Pittsburgh, University of Pittsburgh Press, 1985.

Voorhis, Ernest, *Historic Forts and Trading Posts of the French Regime and of the English Fur Trading Companies*. Ottawa, Department of the Interior, 1930.

Index

Note: alternative fort and place names are given in parentheses. Figures in bold refer to illustrations.